Other *LightLines Publishing* titles:

BOOKS

The Lost Steps of Reiki: The Channeled Teachings of Wei Chi
by Thomas A. Hensel & Kevin Ross Emery

Combing The Mirror (and other steps in your spiritual path)
by Kevin Ross Emery

Experiment Earth: Journey Back To The Beginning
by Kevin Ross Emery & Thomas A. Hensel

Managing The Gift: Alternative Approaches For A.D.D.
by Kevin Ross Emery

AUDIO TAPES

The Lost Steps of Reiki: Transforming An Ancient Healing Art
by Thomas A. Hensel & Kevin Ross Emery

Prosperity & Manifestation
by Thomas A. Hensel & Kevin Ross Emery

The Channeled Messages of Simon Peter
by Thomas A. Hensel & Kevin Ross Emery

COMPACT DISCS

Creating Your Invisible Armor
with Thomas A. Hensel & Kevin Ross Emery

VIDEO TAPES

Managing The Gift: Alternative Approaches For A.D.D.
a six hour workshop with Kevin Ross Emery

Invisible Armor

Protecting Your Personal Energy

Thomas A. Hensel

Edited by
Hillary W. Smith

LightLines Publishing
Portsmouth, NH

Invisible Armor: Protecting Your Personal Energy

First edition, 2000

Published by:

LightLines Publishing
One Middle Street
Portsmouth, NH 03801-4301

E-mail: LightLinesPub@aol.com
Website: http://www.weboflight.com/publish.htm

Manufactured in Canada

ISBN 1-890405-03-5

To Kevin, the true and only love of my life.

To my mother, my best friend and my greatest inspiration.

To my grandmother, the most beautiful and amazing person I have yet to know.

And finally, to the memory of my father, who taught me about quiet strength and the power of living your truth without the need to ever apologize for who you are.

I love you all more than I can truly express on paper.

Acknowledgements

I extend my sincere thanks to all of the people who shared their lives with me to help in the creation of this book . . . clients, students, friends and family. All of you created the energy that manifested this book through me, and the work has always been for you.

Special thanks go to my editor, Hillary Smith, for her knowledge, humor, patience and incredible eye for detail.

Additional thanks to Jodi Barnes, Dara Jane Brennan, Maddie S.G. Cohen, Tricia Dawson, Kevin Ross Emery, Mary Goodman, Arlyn Grant, Mary B. Hensel, Alice Eve Lavelle, Eibhlin MacIntosh, Pat Marggraf, Laurie Paul, Sue Redkey, Scott Richardson, Barbara Roberts and Laura Robinson.

And extra special thanks to the *Woo Squad* . . . with you I truly began the journey to find myself. Love, Light and Laughter!

Tommy Hensel
Portsmouth, NH
March 2000

Contents

Invisible Armor

Protecting Your Personal Energy

*Energy is the only life and is from the Body;
and Reason is the bound or outward circumference of Energy.*

Energy is Eternal Delight.

— William Blake, from *The Marriage of Heaven and Hell*

Introduction

All my life, I have been one of those people to whom others have come to discuss their problems. As a child and a teenager, this was seldom a problem. I enjoyed offering advice, which usually played out as being extremely valuable and accurate.

Things began to change when I went to college. Up to that point, I had lived a very sheltered life. My neighborhood was a typical, homogenous, upper-middle class suburb. Even though I had a large family, there was very little need to share bedroom space, and I had a private room for most of my early life. The school I attended for twelve years was a small, private one with only eighty-five people in my graduating class. What a culture shock it was to suddenly move to a 25,000-person university in another state; to live in a dormitory and share space with hundreds of other people from an incredible diversity of backgrounds!

Into the second semester of my freshman year, I began to exhibit signs of depression. Although there was no real discernible cause, I had definite and protracted periods of emotional sadness. As things progressed into the sophomore year, these depressions began to alternate with times of almost manic positivity. Finally, a concerned friend kidnapped me and drove me to see a psychiatrist — another intimidating experience! Imagine your most stereotypical vision of a psychiatrist, and you would describe him: a tall, very large bearded man sitting behind a giant mahogany desk in a dark paneled office. After just one session, he pronounced that I was likely manic-depressive and would do well to begin taking medication. I refused, unwilling to risk the potential negative side effects of heavy medication.

For several more months, the symptoms continued until the same well-meaning friend kidnapped me again. This time, she took me to a different psychiatrist — a pleasant and charming younger woman who instantly put me at ease. In her work she had become quite an expert on manic-depression. After the session, she informed that while I mimicked the symptoms somewhat, she did not believe that I had clinical manic-depression. Relieved, I gracefully bowed out of continuing therapy and went on with my life.

As many of you have discovered, the universe occasionally drops a solution into your life at the most interesting of times and in the most incongruous of ways. About two weeks after this second round of psychiatry, I sat down at a cafeteria table with a girl I knew casually from one of my classes. Out of the blue, in the middle of a completely unrelated conversation, she turned to me and said, "Oh! You're an unshielded empath."

I am sure the incredulous expression on my face would have made any of you laugh. It took a moment for me to formulate a response, something like, "Excuse me? Could you speak in English?" She proceeded to explain that I was extremely open emotionally and psychically. So open, in fact, that I went through life like a sponge, soaking up the emotions of everyone around me. With the possible exception of a psychiatric hospital, I defy you to imagine many worse places to be an emotional sponge than in a dormitory full of hormonally raging 19-year-old college students!

As it turned out, my friend was a very talented intuitive healer who supplemented her tuition by doing psychic readings. She gave me some simple visualization techniques, which helped me to shield my energy. From then on, my manic-depressive episodes transformed into "normal" college-age emotional fluxes. After a while, I no longer consciously worked with the shielding. Not until many years had passed did I revisit them.

By my early thirties, I had begun a practice as a spiritual counselor and coach. As I worked with people who came to me for a variety of issues, a pattern began to emerge. Every single client had a problem at times being an emotional sponge. Not just a percentage of them, but *every* client! Recognizing their need for energetic self-defense, I revisited my years in college, resurrected the shielding techniques, adapted them for my clients and began to train others in the techniques included in this book. I expanded my practice to include classes and workshops and witnessed significant results in almost every client.

As I worked with people, I noticed that simply trying to put up energetic barriers was not enough. Other issues needed to be addressed. For instance, I began to look at what elements of someone's personality help to co-create these energetic drains? As I worked with hundreds of people, both singly and in groups, it occurred to me that while most people were excellent at understanding what they did *not* wish to have in their lives, few had a clear focus on what they *did* want! In addition, only the tiniest fraction of people seemed to have a grasp of *why* they wanted or did not want these things. Without clarity, they were creating extremely ambiguous signals that did not adequately express their true boundaries.

As I continued training people, I discovered that there was even more involved in creating this energetic protection. To create boundaries is one thing, but to learn how to enforce them in your life is quite another. This was the missing piece of the puzzle. While changing your mental and emotional patterning is the first step in learning to protect your personal energy, true protection comes from understanding, clarifying and *enforcing* your boundaries while learning how to make positive, active change. This change includes issues of altering your boundaries, communicating those changes to others, and dealing with the inevitable responses and reactions from those in your life to the "new you."

The techniques in this book will help you create invisible yet powerful energetic boundaries — what I call "invisible armor." There are two imperatives in doing this work. The first is *simplicity*. Too many people turn self-help and spiritual transformation into the equivalent of rocket science. The elements discussed and explored in this book are specifically designed to be concise and simple. After all, if you cannot use the information *today*; if it cannot make your life better *today*, then what is the purpose? Everyone who reads this book should be able to understand, integrate and apply the concepts in such a way as to make immediate, positive change in their lives.

Of course, no book can solve your problems for you. No ethical author would make those claims. You must commit to doing the work yourself. This leads to the second perspective: *action*.

Information without action is useless. You can analyze something until you have discovered every nuance of its truth, but if you do not take the actions needed to bring that truth into reality, then you have simply wasted your time. This book is filled with experiential exercises designed to help you integrate these concepts into your life. That active step is completely up to you. If you read this book, find it holds some truth for you, and then put it on the shelf to gather dust, then I thank you for your money, but you have just wasted it. However, if you seize the courage to act, you will find that the principles discussed in this book will help you clarify and create a life that brings you greater peace and joy.

The work of creating and maintaining "invisible armor" follows a three-part process mirrored in the structure of this book. Chapters 1–4 teach you to understand energy and its nature. Chapters 5–7 contain practical insights and exercises to help you decide what you want, what you do not want, and how to create the shields to help you achieve those things. Chapters 8–10 detail the follow-up work that will help you communicate and enforce your new truths with the significant others in your life.

I have included several components to clarify the work in this book. You will notice the following as you read further:

Definitions: Many terms have multiple meanings or ambiguous interpretations. All too often, we fall back on "catch words" or popular jargon with little clear understanding of what they really mean. For such terms, I have included a working definition from my perspective. In this way, everyone can be clear as to the meaning being discussed. The book also contains an appendix which lists all of the words defined in the text, as well as a few more which relate to the subject matter.

Exercises: Many of the important concepts include exercises, offering you the chance to actively experience them. Remember that "information without action is useless." These exercises serve as the vehicles to help you make active change by applying the concepts to your daily life. I suggest that you stop whenever you reach an exercise and take the time to do it fully. Also, as the exercises are meant to build one on another, you will reduce the effectiveness if you read ahead too far to see where each is headed.

Homework: The dreaded word! My partner, Kevin Ross Emery, often refers to homework as the "longest four-letter word." In fact, it is two four-letter words in one. As with the exercises, however, these assignments act as focusing tools to help you achieve the long-lasting changes you desire in your life. I suggest reading the book through once, doing the exercises, and then returning to those sections that apply to your specific issues and doing the homework assignments that draw you. To maximize the benefits of the homework, you will probably want to invest in a large journal or notebook. My preference is a loose-leaf binder with plenty of notebook paper. That way you can work on the homework without feeling the need to "get it perfect" the first time. Homework can be done on your own time schedule. These tools are helpful, but (unlike the exercises) are not vital to continuing through the book

Visualizations: You do not need to be an expert in meditation to achieve significant results from these exercises. Each guided visualization focuses on a specific energetic concept that is vital to the success of this work. I suggest taping them with pleasant music in the background so that you can play them over again. If that does not appeal to you, then you may purchase the pre-recorded visualizations in CD format from either your local bookstore or directly from this publisher.

*****

A radio interviewer once posed a brilliant question to me. "What do you see," he asked, "as the highest spiritual essence we can achieve as humans? What would that look like?"

"Oh, an *easy* question?" I answered, laughing. "But I actually have an answer to that. I feel that we are all spiritual beings choosing to live out a human existence. As such, our highest spiritual expression is to be fully, one hundred percent human. To have every experience we can have. To feel every emotion we are able to feel, in the moment, without stuffing them down or editing them. Our highest goal is to be in total joy at all times. Joy is not about being happy all the time, or being naive. Joy is about being completely present in the moment, allowing yourself to have your emotions in totality, expressing them fully. You can be joyfully angry, joyfully sad, and joyfully happy. In all these cases, you are experiencing the wonder of being human. This, for me, is the highest spiritual goal. It is what my partner Kevin calls *empowerment*: to live fully in the present moment, being yourself, without apologies."

It is my fondest desire that you all learn to embrace the present moment, clarifying and actualizing those things which lead you to a life in which you are in charge of your own world. Your personal energy is yours. Do not allow anyone else to take it from you!

Much love,
Tommy Hensel

"The allure of energy–its unifying, underlying, omnipresent, multi-faceted, indeed transcendental nature–has been reflected for millennia in the feelings of awe and reverence connected with fire, light, heat, growth, and motion, and for several centuries in intensifying scientific and engineering efforts seeking to unlock the fundamental laws of nature and to expand civilization's mastery of energy flows." [1]

— Vaclav Smil, from *General Energetics: Energy in the Biosphere and Civilization*

Chapter One

The Allure of Energy

Energy.

The word conjures so many various and diverse images. At once both physical and esoteric, the concept of energy has fascinated humankind since the dawn of recorded history and probably predates even that.

What is this mysterious force? This question has been the subject of thousands of hypotheses over thousands of years. All ancient cultures have conducted experiments with fire, light, heat, motion and other physical phenomena. On the more esoteric side, these same cultures delved deeply into mysticism, spirituality and the nature of the cosmos. Up through the early Christian era and into the Middle Ages, energy was a spiritual concept. All things were thought of as part of the divine energy. To the mystic, energy was and is a force that pervades all things, something that defies categorization and description.

The dawning of the modern age of science brought a shift in perspective. Energy began to be approached in a purely clinical manner as a measurement of work. In fact, the word itself is derived from the Greek meaning "in-work"–the capacity for doing work.

Energy became a subject for physicists and practitioners of the "hard" sciences.

Not until the twentieth century do we see a tentative fusion of these seemingly opposite concepts. Many people look at quantum physics as the ultimate fusion of science and mysticism. Although many physicists disagree with this idea, what they do agree with is that something more exists in the universe than that which we can quantify in the laboratory.

Sir Arthur Eddington, one of the pioneers of modern physics, brilliantly captures this elusive concept:

> "Briefly the position is this. We have learnt that the exploration of the external world by the methods of physical science leads not to a concrete reality but to a shadow world of symbols, beneath which those methods are unadapted for penetrating. Feeling that there must be more behind, we return to our starting point in *human consciousness*–the one centre where more might become known. There [in immediate inward consciousness] we find other stirrings, other revelations than those conditioned by the world of symbols . . . Physics most strongly insists that its methods do not penetrate behind the symbolism. Surely then that mental and spiritual nature of ourselves, know in our minds by an intimate contact transcending the methods of physics, supplies just that . . . which science is admittedly unable to give."[2]

Science, mysticism, religion and philosophy have all approached the subject of energy differently. Yet through all the writings and philosophy, all the definitions and arguments, and after all has been defined and quantified, there remains something which is clearly present, but which cannot be easily discerned, measured or, indeed, touched. I call this the "life-force" energy.

This energy surrounds and pervades us at all times. Some would call it God, Goddess, Christ, Allah, Buddha, Creator, Spirit, Yahweh or any of a thousand other names (including "The Force"). For our purposes, let us simply call it the *life-force*. This life-force binds all things together, giving everything a consciousness. It also shifts and flows continuously. We are in a constantly fluid energetic universe, where our energies merge with everything around us. From the standpoint of physics, this is the constant exchange of electrons from atom to atom, as well as the constant exchange of heat. Our bodies continuously interact with the environment, merging our energy with the energy of all things around us.

In order to introduce you to the concept of human energy fields, I will begin with a simple exercise.

*****

Exercise

FEELING THE FLOW

Place your hands palm to palm. Briskly rub your hands together. Now, slowly begin to move them apart. As you do this, focus on the sensations in your palms.

Do you feel a tingling? A heat? A slight pressure? If not, try rubbing your hands together again and closing your eyes, to filter out distractions.

When you feel something, slowly, move your hands apart to see how long you can maintain the recognition of the physical sensations.

*****

Congratulations! You have experienced the first step towards working with your personal energies. Don't be alarmed or discouraged if you felt little or nothing the first time. Many people have to practice for quite some time before they have discernible, physical sensations.

Now that we have defined energy, we must begin to examine the properties of this force. These are what I call the *Universal Laws of Energy*.

UNIVERSAL LAW # 1: *Energy moves through intention*

Your life-force energy is essentially non-specific. It pervades you and the space around you, yet requires conscious direction to determine where it goes and what it does.

Let us try another exercise.

*****

Exercise

FOCUSING YOUR ENERGY

Once again, place your hands palm to palm. This time, however, close your eyes. Take a deep breath and visualize a column of energy flowing into the top of your head. As you release your breath, picture the energy in your head. Address the energy and direct it to flow down your arms and out of the palms of your hands. See the flow in your mind's eye as it pours into your head and then down your arms and into your hands.

Briskly rub your hands together. Picture the energy in your hands and direct it to flow out of your palms. Slowly begin to move your hands apart. As you do this, focus on the sensations in the palms of your hands. As you feel any strengthening of energy between your hands, allow your hands to move further apart, still maintaining an awareness of the physical sensations.

Did your hands move further than they did in the previous exercise? Did the energy feel different?

*****

This time, most people find that their hands move farther

apart than before. This is an example of the conscious directing of energy. The flow entered your body and you told it where to go. In a similar fashion, you can direct many kinds of energy with your thoughts and conscious awareness, most specifically that life-force energy that surrounds you and makes up your personal space.

Even the Federal Government of the United States has grudgingly begun to accept this esoteric concept. The National Institute of Health currently defines an entire family of therapeutic techniques that they call "biofield therapeutics." They state, "There is a consensus among practitioners that the biofield permeates the physical body and extends outward for several inches. *Extension of the external biofield depends on the person's emotional state and health.*"

UNIVERSAL LAW # 2: *What you send out comes back.*

Every spiritual tradition has taught some variation of this law. In the Christian tradition, we hear, "Cast your bread upon the water and it shall be returned to you ten-fold," and "Do unto others as you would have them do unto you." Also, "Love thy neighbor as thyself." All of these underline the energetic component of the physics truth that "like attracts like."

Energy simply is. It is neither positive nor negative until someone or something provides that focus. In the words of a common saying, "Nothing is either good or bad, but thinking makes it so." When you send out a thought, emotion or action, the intent behind the sending determines the quality. For example, imagine yourself standing on a street corner. On the opposite corner you witness the following events. Two people meet, they speak for a moment and one suddenly slaps the other on the back, knocking him down. Was this negativity? Was this a negative action? Here we run into two of the most misunderstood and ambiguous terms that are applied to energy –the words "negative" and "negativity."

For the purposes of this book, I define them this way:

NEGATIVE: *Energy that is receptive rather than active.*

NEGATIVITY: *Energy intentionally designed to cause harm.*

From a physics standpoint, negative energy must exist so that all things can have balance. Without a negative end, a battery will not work. Electrons will not move. No juice, no energy. Just as we accept the idea that energy exists, we also accept the idea that physical energy has positive and negative polarity. Positive energy projects outward and negative pulls inward in a constantly evolving flow. When dealing with the interaction of your personal energy with the energy around you, however, this definition need not concern you consciously.

To be sure, there are times and experiences which feel "off" or "wrong" to you. You may even experience unpleasant sensations or emotions around certain people, or in certain situations or locations. However, these experiences are not essentially negative by our working definition of the term. Instead, these feelings and sensations are your personal responses to the stimuli, not the direct result of an intentional sending of energy.

For the purposes of discussing the interaction of personal energy we must move to the definition of "negativity," a definition that implies conscious direction. Earlier, I defined "negativity" as "energy that is intentionally designed to cause harm." With this definition in mind, return to the scenario outlined above. Play it through twice with some new information. First, the two people meet. One thinks, "I really hate him and I hope this hurts." With that, he slaps the first man on the back. Positive or negative? By the definition above, this action has a negative energy because it was intentionally directed to cause harm.

Next, play the scene through this way: The two people meet. The first man begins to choke on something he is eating. The second man thinks, "I must help him. He might choke to death." With that, he slaps the first man on the back. Positive or negative? By the definition above, this action has a positive energy because it was intentionally directed to create healing.

To you, the observer, both scenes look exactly the same. To the recipient of the slap, the pain was the same both times. The energy, however, was totally different based on the motivation of the person taking the action. This illustrates a fundamental point in working with energy. You must be clear about both the intention (what you wish to do) and the motivation (why you wish to do it).

The "what" usually comes easily. In the examples above, the second man intended to slap the first man on the back. The "why," however, requires more conscious thought. More on that later.

Both of the Universal Laws of Energy play a significant role in the creation and maintenance of energetic boundaries. When we reach Chapter 7 and learn to create specific and powerful shields, these laws will become of paramount importance. Before we delve more deeply into them, however, I am going to give you a simple yet effective visualization to begin the process of helping you shield your energy right now.

First, a few words about visualization. When you focus your intention very clearly, you send out energy that magnetizes itself to similar energy. In the Second Universal Law of Energy, we discussed the concept that what you send out comes back to you. With his law in mind, you can understand how your visualizations create energy on many levels in order to draw to you what you desire.

The act of visualization works simultaneously on the physical, emotional, intellectual and spiritual levels to help you manifest these desires. Physically, visualizations relax and allow you to create specific visual images. Emotionally, they create feelings of peace and harmony. Intellectually, they help clarify and focus your thoughts. Spiritually, they provide a specific framework within which you contain esoteric, spiritual concepts.

You do not need to be able to meditate to achieve significant results in creative visualization. I cannot meditate without great concentration. Whenever I attempt to rest and meditate, I invariably fall asleep. As a result, the visualizations I have created here and later in the book are geared towards people like me–those who want a fast and effective tool that does not require study or intense concentration.

Before beginning, you will want to focus for a moment on your spiritual belief system. In the visualization, I create a point where you ask for guidance and protection from an outside source. Do you define this source as God, Goddess, Christ, Allah, Buddha, Spirit, Master, Great Spirit, Creator or some other name? Do you work with angels or spirit guides? Stop for a moment and clarify for yourself who and/or what you wish to work with you in the creation and maintenance of your protective shields.

This exercise is split up into two separate visualizations. The first guides you to create a sacred space, a place in your mind's eye where you can travel when you meditate or visualize. The second helps you to cleanse your energy and surround yourself with general protection. In this step, you may wish to draw upon the higher power or powers with which you work to aid and protect you. These two visualizations can easily be done together as one continuous visualization.

Again, I suggest that you either record these words in your own voice, have someone record them for you, have someone read to you when you practice them, or purchase the CD which accompanies this book. The CD contains gentle, soothing background music. For any of the other methods, you may wish to find music of your own. For now, simply read the words slowly and allow yourself to envision as you read.

If possible, prepare yourself and your space to do these visualizations. Find a peaceful room and a comfortable chair. You may also do any of the visualizations while resting in bed or on a couch. Adjust the lighting to create a peaceful, relaxing environment. Beyond the music, you might also wish to light candles, burn incense or aromatherapy or do anything else that helps you relax. I also suggest that you turn off any telephones, beepers or pagers that might distract you.

Once you are in place and the environment is comfortable you are ready to begin.

*****

SACRED SPACE VISUALIZATION

Settle into a comfortable position. Close your eyes and begin slowly breathing in through your nose and out through your mouth. Concentrate on the deepness of your breath, feeling the air come deeper and deeper into your body. Release it by pushing the air out gently.

Allow yourself to breathe in the light and love and energy of this room. Allow yourself to release any ten-

sion, concerns or stress you have accumulated throughout the day. As you breathe in deeply and release, feel
yourself relax deeper and deeper into your own body.
Concentrate on your breath. Breathe in light and love,
hope and serenity. Release negativity and stress. As
you exhale, breathe out all of the "could haves," "should
haves" and "would haves" of your day, of your week.

Now, in your mind's eye, you will begin a journey. Envision yourself in a very large field. To the right of you
is a forest path that leads to a lake. To the left is a path
that will take you up to the mountains. Behind you is a
field of flowers, scattered with trees and rocks. In front
of you is a road that will take you to the edge of the sea.

Look at each road and carefully decide where you would
like to build a sacred space. Do you want it high up in
the mountains? Do you want it in the valley among the
flowers? Do you want it in the caves that lie between
the field of flowers and the mountains? Do you want it
in the forest? Do you want it at the edge of the lake?
Would you like it at the beach? Would you like it on the
cliffs where the beach meets the mountains?

Decide now what place at this moment, at this time in
your life, feels most sacred to you, feels most like home.
Choose that path now. Begin to walk until you find the
perfect place in which to build your sacred space.

As you come to that perfect place, the place which feels
more like home than any home you have ever imagined,
feels more right than any place you have ever been,
welcome any spirit guides or spiritual beings who guide
and protect you on your journeys. Invite them into this
place and they will keep your sacred space for you when
you are not there.

As you create the details of your sacred space, envision

what will feel sacred to you. Will is just be a sacred fire and a place to sit? Will it be a temple? Will it be a castle with walls? Will it be a home with many windows looking over the water? Is it a cabin? Is it a mansion? Is it a rock or is it a cave?

It is a place where you go and only those whom you invite in may come to you there. A place that is sacred. A place of your own Divine. As you create the space, know you can always change it, that you can always come back to it once you have left it. It is yours and it will forever be yours whenever you need to visit a sacred place.

As you finish defining your sacred place, allow yourself to relax as the heavens open. There is a light misty rain, and a still, sunny day, as you stand in the center of the sacred place. And as a gentle rain falls, it surrounds the place and enfolds it. The bright sun is shining and all of the area around your sacred space is swirling with rainbows.

As you sit there, the rain ends, yet the rainbows are still there. The sun grows long in the day and a bright, full moon comes and adds her blessing, illuminating you and your sacred space. Ask for one message now from Spirit, one message to guide you at this, the most important time of your life. For now, the present, this moment as every moment, is the most important time of your life.

Take several moments to sit quietly and get whatever message Spirit has for you. ✱✱

Now it is time to come back. There are no locks, there is no way to secure this place, for this place may not be entered except by you and by Spirit and any whom you shall invite. Leave it now, knowing it is there for you always. Blessed and protected.

Begin to follow the path back to where you started. Come back to the place from which you began this journey.

Take a deep breath and release.

Open your eyes.

*****

Practice this visualization as often as you desire, until you become comfortable with it. Make any specific alterations you need in order to have it feel harmonious with your energy. Once you have become comfortable with this *Sacred Space* visualization, you may choose to continue on to the *Cleansing and Protection* visualization that follows. If you wish to combine the two visualizations, end the *Sacred Space* visualization at the double asterisk (**) and connect that point with the double asterisk in the *Cleansing and Protection* visualization that follows.

*****

CLEANSING AND PROTECTION VISUALIZATION

Settle into a comfortable position. Close your eyes and begin slowly breathing in through your nose and out through your mouth. Take a nice deep breath in, and release. Allow yourself to focus in on your breathing.

Each time you inhale, feel yourself fill with energy. As you exhale, allow yourself to sink deeper and deeper into comfort. Allow the tension and thoughts of the day to simply float away out of your mind with each exhalation.

In your mind's eye, envision yourself in your sacred space. Take a moment to see the sights around you: the beauty of nature, the sky, any plants or animals that happen to be there. Smell the aroma of the growing plants and flowers. If you are near the ocean, smell the salt air. Feel the warmth of the sun on your face and body. A gentle breeze lightly caresses you as it flows by. You can almost taste the pristine, pure air. As you focus around you, you can also hear the light play of the breeze, the sound of birds. Everything is beautiful and clean.
✳✳

As you stand in this beautiful place, envision yourself being showered in energy. It is coming from above you and it gently flows down, flows over your head, flows down your body. You feel yourself bathed in this beautiful energy.

As the energy flows down you, you feel all of the tension melting out of your body. As you look at yourself, you begin to see the toxins releasing. All of the external and internal things that have stuck to you, or stuck in you, are releasing out of you. And the Earth is accepting them as they flow away.

You feel clean and pure and lighter than you have ever felt before, as all of these things simply flow off you, flow out of you and release. Allow yourself to bathe in this beautiful, warm energy as it continues to gently wash over you and release all things from you that are not harmonious.

Slowly, you feel the energy begin to slow down. It is not flowing as strongly. Now it is just a trickle, for you are as clean as you can be. You feel light and buoyant. You feel alive and vibrant. You feel clean and pure.

In this state, invite any beings who guide you–the spirit

guides, the higher powers, whoever it is–to join you. Feel yourself surrounded in beautiful, loving energy. You are clean, you are pure and you have been joined by beautiful loving beings who support you.

In your mind's eye, envision yourself surrounded by a bubble of iridescent, light. You find that in your lightness you have raised off of the ground and you are floating a few inches above the Earth. The bubble of energy surrounds you on all sides, above and below. You are encased in a beautiful bubble of sparkling, iridescent energy.

At this time, ask that this bubble shield and protect you. Ask that it draw to you only those things that are harmonious for you at this time in your life. Ask that anything which will not support you and help you be reflected away with love. Ask the beings who have joined you to help you to maintain this beautiful bubble. They will add their own energies to it.

As you send this thought out, you see each of these beautiful beings whom you have called to you begin to shimmer and glow. As they begin to shimmer and glow, they lose their form and they become pure light. Their energies slowly approach you and begin to merge into the bubble. Now, it is not just an iridescent bubble, it is sparkling with gold and silver and every color of the rainbow as these pure beings have combined their essence to help shield and protect you.

You feel light and buoyant and vibrant and joyful. You feel yourself tingling as these energies merge. Love and protection surround you. Know that only those things that are harmonious at this time in your life will come to you. Any energy that is intentionally directed at you in order to harm you will be reflected back to the sender with love so that they might learn and grow.

With these joyful thoughts, you begin to feel the bubble of energy moving inward towards you, slowly beginning to encompass you. The energy is touching you now and is conforming to the shape of your body like a second skin. You have internalized this energy of protection. All of this energy of the universe from the beautiful loving beings and from your own intention are merged with you. From now on, you will carry your shields and protection within you at all times. You may expand the energy outward, or you may bring it in as you will, but it is now a part of you and can never be separate. You are one with the energy of the Universe. You are one with the energies of joy and love. You are shielded and protected. You are loved.

Allow yourself to feel your body as you come back down to the ground. As your feet touch the Earth, you begin to feel its energy flowing up through the soles of your feet, slowly beginning to energize you again and bring you back to the room. Your feet begin to tingle. The energy of the Earth travels slowly up your legs to your knees, up your thighs to your hips.

You feel the energy of the Earth begin to travel up your torso to your chest. Your arms come back to life and you slowly begin to feel the energy reaching your face. You can feel the muscles in your face coming back. You feel the energy reach your head and as it swirls through your head, you feel it come to your eyes.

When you are comfortable, open your eyes and return once again to the room.

*****

Practice this visualization as often as you desire, until you become comfortable with it. Make any specific alterations you need in order to have it feel harmonious with your energy. Once you have become comfortable with this *Cleansing and Protection* visualization, I suggest that you use it at least once per day, either in conjunction with the *Sacred Space* visualization or alone.

Once you have created your sacred space, you may find that you do not need to do that particular visualization again. At first, however, you will probably want to practice both of these visualizations (or the combined visualization) at least twice a day for about two or three weeks. After that time, drop back to once per day for another two or three weeks. When that period is done, do the visualizations whenever you feel the need to cleanse your energy.

I laughingly remind my clients of a scene in the movie *Ghostbusters*. In a hotel corridor, Bill Murray's character has a ghost fly toward and through him. He shouts, "I've been slimed!" We all feel "slimed" from time to time as we move through our daily lives, those occasions when we feel a little "off" or slightly "unclean." At such times, do these visualizations in order to cleanse your energy and re-shield/re-center yourself

These visualizations are what I call "techniques that are designed to do away with themselves." They are a little like driving a car. When we first learn to drive, we have a long list of items that we must slowly accomplish before moving the car. You enter, put on the seatbelt, adjust the mirrors, check the gauges, insert the key, start the motor, allow it to warm up, look all around, look behind and slowly back up. Today, not a single one of us takes the time to do all of those things consciously, yet all of them get done in the matter of a few seconds. Those techniques that we had to learn when we were in the learning process now have "done away with themselves" and have been internalized so that they are nearly automatic. The same will occur with these shielding techniques after practicing for a while.

These particular visualizations create powerful, but non-specific shields. Later, in Chapters 5–7, you will learn to specify and focus these shields to make them totally your own. In the meantime, now that you are well shielded for the moment, we will examine how the life-force energy functions within and around each of us.

" . . . it is useful to maintain a concept of personal space, which has also been described as a portable territory, since the individual carries it with him wherever he goes."[3]

— Robert Sommer, from *Personal Space: The Behavioral Basis of Design*

Chapter Two

Portable Territory

The life-force energy pervades us, certainly, but it also surrounds us. Just as a gravitational field surrounds a heavenly body, so too does a field surround us. This field is our *personal* life-force field.

Many cultures throughout the centuries have delved into the subject of life-force energy, describing how it surrounds and connects all things. In India, ancient writings refer to the *prana.* In China, we see references to the *ch'i* or *qi.* The Jewish Kabbalah calls this energy *nefish,* and discusses an iridescent bubble that surrounds the human body. This energy was *pneuma* to the Greeks, *arunquiltha* to the Australian aborigine, *ankh* to the Egyptians. In modern writings, we find many references to the *aura.* Today, we often refer to this concept simply as our "space."

How many of you remember that classic phrase, "You're in my space, man"? In the late 1960s and early 1970s, an entire generation of people began to deconstruct and reconstruct our awareness of territory and space. For a period of time, portions of society attempted to return to a tribal sense of being, where the individual space between people was reduced. Even today, we see situations where boundaries are almost non-existent: rock concerts, dance clubs, sports events, parades, etc.

In the majority of situations, however, each one of us has a certain distance surrounding our bodies, a distance that we would define as our "space." Anyone who enters that field without permission we consider to be invading that space. In psychology and sociology, there is a study called "proxemics," the study of interpersonal space and personal boundaries. The term "proxemics" was coined by noted sociologist Edward Hall who postulated that people interact in four categories of personal distance:

Intimate Distance (1–18 inches)

Personal Distance (1 ½–4 feet) – the most common.

Social Distance (4–12 feet) – characterizing business and general social contacts.

Public Distance (12–25 feet) – primarily for formal occasions, public speaking or to create distance for a person of "high" status.

While an invasion of personal space certainly occurs through physical encroachment, it can also be created by the invasion of the other senses. Eye contact, loud noises, unpleasant odors and disharmonious visual images all affect our energy, creating a sense of personal violation. As might be expected, different situations mandate different boundaries. Jonathan Freedman, a respected researcher of proxemics, notes, " . . . the appropriate distance depends almost entirely on such factors as the relationship among the people, the setting, and the personal characteristics of those people."[4]

Cultures, too, have widely divergent spatial needs. In Hong Kong, for instance, crowding has created a culture whose personal space requirements are much smaller than in the United States. Many Middle Eastern and some European cultures seem to have far more comfort being physically close than we do in the United States. Conversely, many Far Eastern cultures find our Western idea of making eye contact to be incredibly intrusive. What seems clear, however, is that all people, regardless of culture or situation, have a certain field which surrounds them and moves with them, what Robert Sommer calls *portable territory*.[5]

The boundaries of your portable territory are not symmetrical. It has been my observation that more space exists in front of a person than behind, almost as though you were standing inside of an egg, with the body at the small end of the egg. Because vision extends in front and, to a certain extent, to the periphery, your spatial boundaries are greater there. Behind you, the boundaries are closer. Most researchers into proxemics estimate that the average American requires from eighteen inches to two feet of personal space. I would alter that to extend approximately two and one half feet in front, wrapping around to about one foot in back in the egg-shape.

What linear studies have not taken into account is the nature of the energy that creates personal space. In the earlier chapter, you explored and contacted you own personal energy. You then learned how to project that energy. Understanding these things, you will see that your personal space is more than an abstract distance. It is a field of energy that flows from you and surrounds you, an extension of your own mind, emotions and spirit, the "living force emanated by consciousness."[6]

With this perspective, let us pose a question. If you require two feet of space and a person who approaches you also requires two feet of space, where do you begin to feel their energy? If you said, "At four feet," then you are right on the mark. At that distance, your own field contacts theirs, creating a mixture of personal energies. If those energies are harmonious, then you will both feel comfortable. If one energy does not mix well with the other, one or more of the parties will feel some measure of discomfort. These feelings may be, and probably will be, very subtle and primarily emotional. The discomfort, though, is very real.

One manner in which to cope with such issues is to remember your ability to focus and direct your personal energy. As the mystic and poet William Blake wrote, "Energy is the only life and is from the Body / and Reason is the bound or outward circumference of Energy." Your directed, intentional thoughts (i.e. Reason) determine the boundaries of your energy. Just as you directed that flow out of your hands, you can also expand and contract your personal energy fields. Many people do this quite unconsciously.

I was once at a rather elegant cocktail party in Washington, DC. The room was full of dignitaries, politicians, ambassadors and various other high-profile social types. As you can imagine, the energy was quite chaotic and unfocused. I was facing the door, while many people were at the buffet with their backs to the entrance. Suddenly, the door opened and a noted Hollywood celebrity entered, unnoticed visually by most of the people in the room. To my surprise, however, with no visual clues a number of people at the buffet turned around to face the door only two or three seconds after the celebrity entered.

Coincidence? Not at all. When that woman entered the room, her energy expanded to fill it. Her level of self-confidence and her surety that she could and would be the center of attention preceded her and touched the energy of every person there. Once she was present, and had been "seen," her energy receded to a normal distance and she began making the rounds of the party. The power of her presence came from an almost instinctive pushing out of her personal energy, figuratively "tapping everyone on the back" to make them turn and look.

The opposite is also possible. When I spend time in airports, I find the frenetic and often frustrated energy to be nearly overwhelming. As a result, I will search for a distant (usually a corner) seat. I quietly settle in, pull in my energy and direct it to blend me in with the wall. In this way, you can become essentially "invisible" to most people who are in chaotic, self-directed energy flows. This technique is a type of protection, as well as a wonderful tool for people watching! And that, in fact, is your first homework exercise.

*****

Homework

OBSERVATION OF PERSONAL SPACE

Over the next several days, observe people in a variety of public situations. Some perfect places to observe are airports, bus terminals, train stations, doctor's offices, supermarkets, malls, department stores and city sidewalks. Note how people enforce their personal space needs. How do they position themselves? How do they react when others get too close?

At the end of each day, take a few minutes to journal on your observations. Did you discern any regular patterns? Did you notice any outstanding or interesting moments? Did you notice any changes in your own space needs as a result of these observations?

Begin to become more aware of when you expand and contract your personal space. With whom do you feel safe enough to allow close contact? With whom to feel the desire to create greater distance? Note these observations in your journal.

*****

One area in which our modern world has created a specific set of space issues is in the area of driving. Road rage has become increasingly more common. There are many people doing a great deal of psychological research on this unfortunate phenomenon. From an energetic perspective, there could be another explanation.

In our lives, we often feel powerless in one way or another. When we get behind the wheel of a car, however, we are in control. Our personal energy encompasses that vehicle and, in essence, it becomes an extension of us. Thus, the car begins to have boundaries that extend several feet on all sides, primarily in the front and back. When another driver pulls up behind us, or cuts us off closely in front, we react just as we would if it happened to us physically walking down the street. Our space is invaded and we most often have an instantaneous reaction of fear and anger.

What else can account for the almost irrational reaction most people have to being tailgated? Certainly it is not safe to follow another car too closely, but most drivers have gigantic anger responses when they perceive in the rear-view mirror that someone is too close. In his discussion of spatial invasion, proxemics researcher Robert Sommer notes, "A driver can make another exceedingly nervous by tailgating. Highway authorities recommend a 'space cushion' of at least one car length for every ten miles per hour of speed."[7]   Under these circumstances, even the most docile of drivers can move from calm to rage in a few seconds.

So . . . another homework exercise.

*****

Homework

ON THE ROAD AGAIN

As you travel, whether as driver or passenger, notice the interplay of boundaries on the road. When you drive, notice your own energetic reactions to other vehicles. Do you have large reactions to minor things? Do others establish and enforce clear spatial boundaries? Do you? How do you perceive the reactions of other drivers? In your estimation, are they being irrational?

Pay attention to where you are allowing others to manipulate your energy through violation of boundaries. This perception will carry over very well into later exercises about your personal physical boundary issues.

You might notice, as well, that similar energies hold in the supermarket as on the highway! People with shopping carts often act as though they were in a car, pushing through everyone else's space without regard. You might want to revisit the "supermarket" portion of Homework #1 and see what you notice.

*****

Although people speak with great humor about their "space–usually making it into a joke–the boundaries are very real. The feelings one has when they are violated are also very real and quite powerful. To notice and define the physical presence and extent of your own personal spatial needs is the first step towards learning how to protect yourself.

Can I see another's woe,
And not be in sorrow too?
Can I see another's grief,
And not seek for kind relief?

— William Blake, from *On Another's Sorrow*

Chapter 3

Fellow Feeling

Thus far we have focused on your personal space from a passive perspective of moving through the world and responding to the stimuli you receive. But what about your active interactions with others? As human beings, we are in constant interaction with all energies around us. Sun, wind, water, plants, animals and stones all exist in a complex web of interrelations. For a human, however, the most powerful connections come with other humans. Two options exist as you move through a world of human interaction: *sympathy* or *empathy*. These two concepts determine whether you will feel empowered or drained when you engage in interpersonal communication.

Sympathy comes from the Greek *sym* (with) + *pathos* (sensation), meaning "to feel with someone." The dictionary includes one definition that calls sympathy "the fact or power of sharing the feelings of another, especially in sorrow or trouble; fellow feeling, compassion or commiseration." This is essentially a passive experience of understanding the emotions of another person without feeling them.

Empathy has a much more fascinating derivation. At the end of the nineteenth century, German aestheticians coined a term *Einfühlungsvermögen* to describe the process of a person projecting himself or herself into a work of art and having an emotional response. *Einfühlung*, the root of this rather lengthy German word, literally means "feeling into." Psychologists appropriated the term, redefining it as "the capacity for projecting oneself into another's mind, achieving a sympathetic understanding of someone." To translate into English, the meaning was applied to the same Greek roots as sympathy, creating *en* (into) + *pathos* (sensation), to feel into another person. Earlier in the 18th century, economist and moral philosopher Adam Smith coined the term "fellow-feeling" to describe this state that we call empathy. Today, the English dictionary defines empathy as "the intellectual identification with or vicarious experiencing of the feelings, thoughts or attitudes of another."

Here we find a definite active component. True empathy results from actively opening up and either projecting your energy into another person or permitting them to project it into you. In either case, the empath feels the emotions in their own physical body *as if these emotions were their own*. Your body does not differentiate between your emotions and those of the person with whom you have established empathy. As a result, you must process and release these emotions as you would your own. Your goal, then, is to become *sym*-pathetic and not *em*-pathetic to avoid a tremendous burden of undesirable energy. As in the William Blake poem that opens this chapter, we must be careful not to take on another's sorrow and make it our own.

The techniques to deal with this type of energetic draining involve some conscious understanding of the dynamics of human relationships. In passive communication, we simply pass through the world and let interactions occur. My adolescent and college years as an "emotional sponge" were essentially years in which I permitted any and all energies to flow into and through me, but with no conscious direction.

When we communicate with another person, however, we engage in an *active* interaction of energies. Verbal, physical, emotional and spiritual energies flow back and forth from person to person. In *The Celestine Prophecy*, James Redfield brilliantly discusses this flow of information, focusing at one point on the actual events that occur when two people begin to communicate purposefully one with the other. I highly recommend reading *The Celestine Prophecy*, or at least those sections on energy exchange.

To merge Mr. Redfield's views with my own experience, let us examine the nature of human interaction. In direct personal communication, each person actively opens his or her energy to the other. Their personal space boundaries intersect and merge. As they communicate, energy flows back and forth. In a positive, empowering situation, each person feeds the other to support and enliven. Each participant feels balanced and centered at the conclusion of the interchange. This type of interaction stems from a definite "win/win" reality. Both parties feel invigorated and positive.

In a direct communication that involves argument or conflict, however, each person opens to the other and attempts to seize power. As the flow moves from person to person, each one grabs and absorbs whatever energy they can. At the end, whoever feels less drained is the "winner." Here we see a clear "win/lose" reality. Both parties feel that they must take something from the other, and the exchange is powerful and often energetically violent. It is not uncommon to feel abused or violated after a confrontational situation, since both parties literally rip energy out of each other by the force of their will.

In many situations, one party enters the exchange with a feeling of being under the power of the other, as in a situation with an abusive employer, or an authority figure such as a police officer or IRS agent. Here, the one who already feels powerless will almost certainly "lose" the energetic battle, since they have a predisposed energy that says, "Here, I'm a smorgasbord. Take whatever you want." Most of us, at some point, have created this scenario based on the fear of being powerless against "the system" or some specific person or situation we feel to be overwhelming.

These types of interactions illustrate the active draining which so many people feel in interpersonal communication. From lover to parent to employer to co-worker to institutional authority figure, we all have at least one experience of someone "sucking us dry" emotionally. Many times, this draining is not from a conscious level.

When someone is in great emotional distress, we have an

almost overwhelming, instinctive response to help them with their pain. Unless we are extremely careful and conscious of our energetic boundaries, however, our desire to help will open up in such a way as to create an empathic drain. The recipient, in need of comfort or balance, will take that energy from the empath. Most vulnerable are those who work in any sort of healing profession. Doctors, nurses, counselors, ministers, massage therapists, energetic healers or anyone who works actively with people in pain must be extremely careful to create sympathy without creating an empathic connection which will surely drain them. Otherwise, you become what my partner Kevin laughingly calls an "energy sundae."

You see a person starving for energy. In your desire to help them, you open yourself up and energetically say to them, "Here I am, a tasty, nutritious energy sundae. Take as much as you want." To the starving person, this energy sundae is a lifesaver. To the sundae, it is a quick way to get sucked completely dry. Once the energy sundae is depleted, what a great empty receptacle it makes to deposit any waste or negative by-products! The starving person, no longer hungry, can then use this receptacle to dump their unwanted emotional garbage.

Another personal example: All my life, I have been my mother's chosen counselor. From my earliest memories, she has come to me to discuss her problems with the other kids, with my father, her sister or her mother. Every time I had a conversation with my mother in which she had some sort of complaint to vent, I would leave the interaction feeling tired! Until I began doing the work detailed in this book, however, I did not make a rather significant logical connection.

My mother never consciously drained me, but I permitted the draining to occur, essentially offering myself up as an "energy sundae." In my desire to be of service, I dropped my boundaries and permitted her to take energy from me and then to unload her emotional distress, her garbage, into me. Afterwards, my emotional body was drained and, as a result, unable to adequately process my emotions *and* my mother's. Remember, *allowing* is not a passive concept. To allow, you must actively and consciously choose to adjust your energetic boundaries.

This idea may seem radical. For so long, society has taught

us that allowing is a passive concept of simply letting things take their course. In the world of spirituality, you constantly hear, "Simply let go and allow." But letting go is an action that requires conscious thought and intention. To allow something to occur, you must make an active choice to adjust your boundaries.

Thus far, we have discussed active, co-creative relationships. Sometimes, however, we have tremendous energetic reactions without the other party actively participating. Rachel, a friend of mine from college, provided me with a fascinating description of her physical reaction to nonspecific, but pervasive feelings of uneasiness, particularly when they emanate from a specific person. In this first example, she discusses her reactions in situations where she must stay around a person and cannot simply leave:

> "When I encounter someone who makes me uneasy, I immediately find my shield going up. All my energy becomes hidden. I show no emotion. I pull myself into myself. It's like sucking my being into the depths of my body. This includes bringing my arms against my side or across my body and not moving in any way. I often think of being in pain when this happens, though I don't feel anything physical. This reaction happens as soon as a 'bad person' enters the room. And it goes away as soon as I or the bad person leaves. When I am no longer in the presence of the person, I feel my entire body relax. I can smile again and feel emotion. I can feel myself extending my feelers."

In this example, Rachel describes an almost total shielding from the surrounding energetic environment. She retreats into a shell and erects shields that approximate iron shells around her. While no energy gets in, very little can get out. But in those moments this particular technique makes her feel safe.

Rachel describes her responses when she encounters a situation that does not require that she physically remain present:

> "Sometimes I find myself with a person who does not give off the 'bad' vibes, but still saps my strength. I

stay away from these people as well. But I haven't noticed my shield automatically going up when I'm with this kind of person. I usually just remove myself from the situation as soon as possible and avoid long exposure to this person."

Here, Rachel does not need to totally shield herself from all surrounding energy. Rather, she has a more primal and simpler response. She leaves! What makes both of these examples worth noting is the inclusion of her release and relaxation. Once Rachel feels "safe" again, she relaxes and allows her normal emotional responses to return. She can feel herself "extending her feelers" again, establishing a healthy, interactive energetic exchange with the world around her.

June, a woman who attended one of my *Invisible Armor* lectures, provides another extremely potent example of feeling forceful energy without the other party actively participating. She recounts the following story about a man on whom she had a tremendous crush:

"Not too long ago, I came out of the back of the store where I work and saw him. I remember looking at him, not feeling the usual energy surge associated with him, but being unable to move or speak. I have very vague memories of what happened after that. I seem to remember he somehow got beyond me and was talking to a really cute little child. I felt intensely hot and flushed and did not want him to see me with my face all red. The next thing I remember is being able to move, think and speak again. I looked around and could not find him or the child anywhere in the store, nor do I have a recollection of them leaving. It was embarrassing to have no recollection and experience such a loss of time."

For June, the intense emotional and physical response occurred as a result of the stimulus of seeing this man. He did nothing active to engage the energy. Her historical relationship with him and her own feelings about the relationship had created a powerful layered energy that released when triggered by his presence. When we discussed the issue, she told me about similar reactions she sometimes had at the mere thought of the man. Again, the other party does not actively engage the energy, but June actively allows herself to perpetuate an unresolved relationship, resulting in potent, sometimes debilitating emotional fluctuation.

This type of emotional drainage occurs frequently in our lives when we have unresolved issues. Simply thinking about a person or situation brings up energy, frequently draining us completely. Although the other party does not consciously participate, their energy does become involved in some fashion. You open up and actively allow your energy to reconnect with theirs on some level, catalyzing the emotional reaction and subsequent feeling of drainage or absorption. Like June, each of us occasionally permits a memory or unresolved emotion to surge back to the forefront of our consciousness, creating a reaction as strong as though the original situation had just occurred.

Earlier, I presented two examples of Rachel dealing with the pervasive energy of specific people. She also describes her experiences when dealing with the nonspecific yet prevalent energy found in public places.

"I have found that whenever I'm out in public, my shield is always up. I have an 'unapproachable' air about me. I lose my peripheral vision. I am closed in around myself. Once I get to where I need to be, and am with people I know and trust, my shielding goes down."

For Rachel, simply moving through the world feels unsafe. As a result, she has learned to create an area of space around herself, one that pushes her personal boundaries out with a specific intention of keeping others away from her. This isolationism may not necessarily be healthy, but it provides a clear example of how someone can experience powerful energy without active thought on the part of the other people involved.

Some physical clues that indicate you may be in a shutdown

mode include: crossing arms over the solar plexus, crossing legs, turning to the side while sitting, wavering eye contact or increasing the physical distance between yourself and another person. You might also feel a curious detachment, a lack of any kind of clear emotion or thought in a situation.

Unfortunately, many people move through the world *intentionally* taking energy from those around them. I term these people "energetic vampires." The legendary vampire must drain the blood of others to maintain his or her life. The "energetic vampire" feels the need to drain the life-force energy of others to create energy for him or herself. These people fall into two categories, *needy* and *energy-addicted*.

The needy vampire leeches your energy by attaching to you and your desire to help. They understand that they feel drained, and know that they always feel better after talking to you. Thus, they come to you with a purpose. Their life is a constant crisis, one trauma after another. They seek you out and vent their problems, asking you to feel sorry for them. Once you open up your energy to them, they attach to you and drain your life-force in order to feed their sense of powerlessness. Once they are "full," they leave you feeling like an empty husk.

The needy vampire is that person in your life who you just "cannot get rid of." You know their visits aggravate you, but you feel sorry for them and, in the words of one client, "I just can't bear the thought of telling her off. She's so fragile. I don't want to be responsible if she goes over the deep end." Skillfully, the needy vampire in this client's life has created in her a permanent "energy sundae bar."

The other category of energy vampirism is the *energy-addicted vampire*. From an esoteric, energetic perspective, the energy-addicted vampire knows exactly what he or she is doing. They do not necessarily feel drained; rather, they have become addicted to the adrenaline that comes with powerful emotion. These people understand emotions in such a way that they can manipulate you to open your energy. One manner in which this occurs is in the guise of sympathy. Suppose you are distraught over something. The energy-addicted vampire approaches you and asks you what's wrong. They then manipulate the conversation to have you *relive* your emotions rather than simply discussing them. Once you are emotionally overloaded, they absorb that energy very much like a drug addict taking a "hit."

The energy-addicted vampires are sometimes those people who move through a world of perpetual crisis, never fully engaged in the crises themselves but always living on the fringes of them. They gravitate towards relationships with people who are volatile, emotional and very often vulnerable and easily manipulated.

Dealing in percentages, only an approximate 10 percent of the people with whom you interact fall into either of the "energetic vampire" categories. The remaining 90 percent of your relationships exist in a world where neither party willfully or consciously drains the other's energy. In my work, however, I do find that an awareness of this possibility helps people to see it when it occurs, facilitating a quicker transformation through these energies.

*****

Thus far we have focused primarily on the effect of other people on you. But what of your effect on others? Each of us has occasion to fall into the role of energy vampire. Examine your personal relationships and honestly assess where you might fit the descriptions given in the preceding paragraphs. Do you have any relationships that might be termed "co-dependent"? If so, remember that co-dependency requires the active participation of both parties, resulting in reciprocal draining of energy.

Before we move on, here is an exercise to help you examine where and how you feel drained in your life, where you drain others and where you feel like an emotional sponge.

*****

Exercise

EXAMINING YOUR LIFE

Examine the major relationships in your life. For each one, create a page in your journal, writing that person's name at the top of the page. Do the same for each major area of your life, being sure to include FAMILY, FRIENDS, INTIMATE PARTNERS, and BUSINESS/WORKPLACE as they apply.

Make three columns on each page. The first will be titled "How I Am Being Drained." The second will be titled, "How I'm Absorbing Unwanted Stuff." (I know . . . the technical terms are staggering, but "stuff" really does describe it better than any other polite term I've tried.) The final column will be titled "How I Am Draining Others."

Examine each relationship or area and begin to make your lists. Any surprises? Next, journal about where you allow these things to occur in your life. Be sure to indicate where you perceive someone is taking your energy willfully, as an "energetic vampire" and where you might be draining someone willfully. Next, examine which relationships are draining even without the active participation of either party. Did you experience any emotions while you were making the lists or journaling? If so, journal a little more on those emotions.

You will use these lists later on, so make sure you keep them in a safe place!

There is spirit in this place,
     Some of this spirit,
Here when I got here,
     Some I brought with me.

Spirited, this place,
     As I am.
Unlike me, however,
     For I move on.

Moving on,
     Spreading Spirit
This place staying here,
     Gathering Spirit, from all who pass.

Giving and taking,
     This place and I,
And some of this spirit I now spread,
     Is this place.

And some of this place's spirit,
     Is from what I left behind.
Taking and giving,
     I and this place.

— Kevin Ross Emery, *Spiritus Loci*

Chapter 4

Spiritus Loci

Most empathic draining is a co-creative process in which you and the other person dance a subtle dance, both participating through *active choice*. But what of your interactions with non-human energy sources? In our universe of energy, we constantly move in and out of the fields of plants, animals, minerals, objects and physical locations. These experiences can be and often are as energetically significant as any interpersonal human relationships.

In the last chapter we discussed the idea that as human beings we are in constant interaction with all energies around us. Sun, wind, water, other people, plants, animals and stones exist in a complex web of interrelations. You absorb and feed energy from yourself to objects just as you do with other people. In return, the objects absorb and feed energy from themselves to you. This exchange can create a palpable energy in a location or an object. The poem that opens this chapter illustrates the powerful concept of *spiritus* or *genius loci*, the spirit of place.

A client, Marguerite, once came to me with an intriguing problem. Her family had recently moved into a much larger and nicer home, allowing each of their children to have a separate bed-room. Her youngest son had particularly hated co-habitating with his older brother and had looked forward to the idea of having his own space. Once in the house, however, this child began to have night-mares and his sleep patterns became very unpredictable. He started to complain about the feeling of his room, the feeling that someone or something was watching him with unpleasant intent.

Marguerite asked me to come to the house, under the assumption that there was an unhappy spirit of some type in the room. She knew that my partner and I had often done spirit release and ghost clearings and assumed this would solve the problem. When I entered the home, I perceived no signs of a spirit in any location, including the bedroom in question. There were, however, very strong and palpable feelings of anger and pain. Opening up to my intuitive, I began to receive messages from the room itself, images of the former occupants. I saw a frightened child, and a man beating that child severely. After spending a little time with these images, I went downstairs to talk to Marguerite.

I asked her if she had any knowledge of the former occupants. In fact, she did. The family had sold the home because of a divorce. The father had been verbally and physically abusive to the wife and children. As a result, the family split up. This validated the messages and images I had received. Over a protracted period of time, the inhabitant of that room, the child, had been repeatedly beaten and abused. Each time, the feelings of anger and pain permeated the room. Time after time, these energies radiated and eventually became embedded in the room itself. We cleared and cleansed the energy of the space, and to my knowledge Marguerite's son is still happily living there, finally getting the private room he desired.

Here you see the generalized energy of space. The constant repetition of emotions and actions literally layered energy into the walls, ceiling and floor. On a less drastic note, this same type of experience often happens when you enter a room after there has been a significant energetic release, such as an argument. You can "feel" the anger in the air. Eventually, this energy dissipates unless it is constantly renewed, as in the above example of the abused child.

The same applies for energy that you might identify as more "positive." Our friend Cheryl once asked Kevin to come and clear a spirit from her home. She was convinced that her grandmother was there, and needed to be gently guided to the other side. When Kevin arrived, he perceived no presence of the grandmother's spirit. When asked to elaborate, Cheryl indicated that she frequently felt a warm, loving emotion that was precisely what she felt when she had spent time with her grandmother.

Kevin went with her to the den. This was the room in which she indicated the feeling to be the strongest. Next to a fireplace was a beautiful antique rocking chair. Standing in that corner and sitting in the chair, Kevin could feel a sense of love, protection and peace. Not a trapped spirit, but a powerful, pervasive positive emotion.

As it turned out, Cheryl had inherited the house from her grandmother. The rocking chair had been in that location ever since she could remember. Her grandmother had held her children and her grandchildren there, she had knitted and read by the fire. For over sixty years, she layered love, protection and nurturing into the walls and into the chair itself. This was the "presence" Cheryl felt. Not the grandmother, but the constant reminder of her loving presence.

In the first story, you see the more generalized energy of a space. In the second, a more specific energy in an object. Both instances were equally powerful in their own way, though very different in quality. These same concepts of energetic absorption and spirit of place often apply to larger spaces as well. Many specific places in the world are believed to be "positive" power points. Locations such as Sedona, Macchu Picchu, the pyramids of Egypt, Stonehenge and others are purported to have powerful energies that can help facilitate transformation.

When you visit such a place, you may feel a shift or change in the feelings around you. This same experience often occurs in secluded forest glades, on the shores of mountain lakes, at the seacoast, or in other areas which are more pristine and protected. In such areas, the energy of nature has been allowed to flourish without toxification. There, you may feel more peaceful, relaxed or centered as a result of this positive energy flow.

Conversely, there are locations that have layers of pain and trauma attached to them. Once such instance served as my most powerful personal example of *spiritus loci*. A number of years ago, I had the joy of backpacking through Europe. One of my favorite cities was Vienna. Over several weeks, I explored much of the Austrian countryside around this beautiful city, finally coming across the town of Dachau. This charming town, of course, has an infamous history as the location of one of the worst of the Nazi concentration camps. I decided to visit the museum and exhibition housed at the remains of this camp.

Initially, the museum and exhibition were disturbing to me because of the enormity of the horrors inflicted in the camp. However, nothing prepared me for the intense wave of emotion that engulfed me when I left the museum and stepped out into the grounds of the camp itself. Over the next two hours, I moved through a fog of energy, very nearly unable to contain the emotions that were trying to come out of me. Never before and never since have I experienced this level of overwhelming energy. The layered emotions of hundreds of thousands of people had embedded into the earth itself. Anger, rage, joy, sadness, hope, fear, pain, anguish . . . everything you could possible imagine as an emotional expression poured over me in a tidal wave. Only after several minutes of intense focus and meditation did I push my shields back out and filter the energy.

Many locations on the planet embody powerful energies created either by the constant repetition of emotion and action or a single cataclysmic event. Places like Dachau, Auschwitz, Hiroshima, Nagasaki and even less obvious places such as the dungeons of European castles or the site of the missing Roanoke Island colony in North Carolina have tangible energy which results in emotional response for those who are not well shielded.

Closer to home, my friend Angela offered the following example of energy in a more specific location. In her words:

"I had an unfortunate experience with taking on the energy of others without realizing what was happening. I had had a wonderful Argentine Tango dance partner who was a 13-year survivor of AIDS. We had the best time going out dancing and taking classes until the disease finally took its toll and he passed away in December of 1997. He had worked for a large metropolitan hospital in their infectious disease department, and had the unpleasant duty of telling people and, many times, their parents, that they were infected with the AIDS virus.

"The memorial service that was held for him

took place at the building where he worked. As I parked and got out of the car, a security guard was coming around the building and asked if I was going to the memorial service. I said I was, so he said he would take me through the building instead of me having to go around to the front where it was being held. As I walked in, a terrible feeling of overwhelming sadness came over me. When I finally got to the front, it was all I could do to keep from sobbing uncontrollably. I managed to get through the service, but left feeling just awful and went on a crying jag that lasted all day. I had loved my friend, but the feeling I had was way out of proportion to what our relationship had been and I couldn't understand it or control it.

"Finally I started calling some of my healer friends because I knew I needed help and found one to work on me. She put her hands on me and immediately said, 'Where on earth have you been?' I told her and then it dawned on me–I had walked through a place filled with horrendous energy of pain and suffering as people were essentially being given death sentences as they discovered they had the AIDS virus. Many times this was the first time that their parents learned that their son or daughter was homosexual and therefore the energy was exceedingly dense, to say the least. I had picked up on all of the grief and turmoil and rage and bitterness that had been expended in the building and it really knocked me for a loop. It took several days to clear it all out and almost constant Reiki sessions by myself and others to get me back to normal. If I had been aware of it, I would have put protection around myself, but it never even crossed my mind. I figured I was going to a funeral and therefore expected to be a little down, but I should have realized from the intensity of the feelings that they weren't mine."

Locations such as hospitals and nursing homes can also serve as powerful receptacles of energy patterns. Angela's response to the energy of the building mirrors my own experiences in dealing with buildings which house repeated powerful energies.

Examine your reactions when entering hospitals, nursing homes, doctors' offices, jails, cemeteries or courthouses. What do you feel? How do your responses and reactions differ from those outside of these locations? Do your physical mannerisms or vocal patterns change significantly? Upon leaving, do you carry any energy with you? These are the kinds of questions that may help you see where you absorb *spiritus loci*.

*****

Homework

SPIRITUS LOCI

Another list-making assignment. Recall any locations where you have felt an extraordinary energy. Focus on those places that created energies in you, but where you had no clear, personal experience to account for the energy.

First, list those places where you felt exceedingly happy, positive or empowered.

Next, list those places in which you felt drained, fearful, angry or disempowered in some manner.

For each thing on your list, journal briefly about the energy. What were the feelings or sensations? Did you have emotional responses, physical responses or both? Did the emotions or sensations stay with you? Did they dissipate when you were no longer in the location? Have

*you had occasion to revisit any of these loca-
tions? Was the energy different at different
times?*

*****

As you move through a world of energetic relationships, you
must examine not only your interactions with other people, objects
and locations, but also with plants and animals. Plants in their
natural habitat give and receive a constant flow of spiritual energy.
The old joke about "hugging a tree" can be a powerful way to help
yourself re-enter that spiritual flow. Rarely have I found a person
receiving distressful energy from a plant, but frequently we project
energy towards them. In a room or a garden in which tremendously
disharmonious emotions abound, plants can and do have a difficult
time thriving. Look to the plant as giving you a message about the
energy of its location.

Animals provide a much clearer object lesson. Domestic
animals generally have one person with whom they are most closely
associated. When that animal develops a noticeable shift in energy,
whether emotional or physical, the animal serves as a message to that
person. Often, we unconsciously look at our pets as our "emotional
garbage cans," using them as a place to dump all of our stress and
pain. Holding the cat or petting the dog helps us release the stress
and feel calmer. For the most part, the animals have the ability to
process this energy and release it. At times, however, they overload
just as we would. In this overload process, examine your own energies and look to the animal as the bearer of a powerful message.
Where are you allowing others to overload you, creating the need to
pass that on to the animal?

As an absorbent object, you passively receive a constant flow
of energy from every object, animal, plant and location with which
you interact. In turn, you constantly radiate energy to everything with
which you come in contact. To repeat the end of the poem that
opened this chapter:

Giving and taking,
This place and I,
And some of this spirit I now spread,
Is this place.

And some of this place's spirit,
Is from what I left behind.
Taking and giving,
I and this place.

Your choices and thought processes determine how much or how little these things affect you as well as how much or little you affect them. So, how do you make different choices? And how do you focus your energy to stop the passive, "emotional sponge" feelings? Let us move on and start digging into the core of this process of energetic self-protection, the creation of your *invisible armor.*

We would often be sorry
if our wishes were gratified.

— Aesop, from *The Old Man And Death*

Chapter 5

Be Careful What You Wish For

Most of us were brought up on fairy tales–the stories of "Snow White," "Cinderella," "Jack and the Beanstalk" and others. In all of these stories, the primary character has a wish, a desire, which eventually comes to pass. In their fascinating musical "Into The Woods," James Lapine and Stephen Sondheim investigate the rest of the story, what happens after the fairy tale wishes have been fulfilled. In each case, the character discovers that his or her wish was perfect for the moment, but in the long run was a mistake. The "perfect" husband turns out to be dull and unfaithful, the long-awaited baby is nothing but trouble, and the death of the giant results in retribution by the giant's wife, creating havoc for all concerned.

We all go through life making wishes, creating desires and fulfilling them, only to discover that they were not appropriate. The old adage, "Be careful what you wish for . . . you just might get it" begins to ring true. But what is wrong with wishing? Nothing! Where we fall short is in the clarity of our desires. You must clearly define what you want.

Here is my favorite story to illustrate this point:

Rose, a friend and fellow spiritual counselor, went through a rather painful break-up. In the aftermath, she swore that she would never again make the same mistakes in a relationship. Towards that goal, she decided to get extremely clear about what kind of man she wished to manifest in her life. Having done a great deal of work with manifestation and the energies of creating the realities of your own life, Rose began as she had taught her clients. She sat down and made a list of what she wanted in a partner.

The first item on her list was, "I want a partner who is a non-smoker." Her former partner had become a chain smoker, and she had developed both an aversion and an allergy to cigarette smoke. She then continued with the other attributes that were important to her. Finishing off her list, Rose then did a ritual in which she burned the paper, offering the energy up to the universe to manifest her perfect mate.

A few weeks later, Rose went out on her first date. The man smoked. Returning from the date, she decided that she had not put enough energy into communicating her desires. She made the list again, and did a longer, more intensive ritual. The second man she dated smoked. And the third. And the fourth. After doing one more round of ritual manifestation, Rose finally went out on a date with a man who did not smoke cigarettes. This one smoked cigars!

Throwing up her hands, Rose lamented that she obviously was not meant to have a partner and that she was also unable to manifest. In her disgust, she began to debate her own ability to do spiritual work. If she could not manifest the first, most simple thing on her list, then how could she teach anyone else to do it?

Often, when we learn to quiet our minds enough, the universe will grace us with inspiration in the form of a still, small voice that speaks to us within. This was Rose's experience. Once she had exhausted her complaining, she heard a gentle voice.

"What were you thinking of when you thought of the phrase "non smoker"?" the voice asked.

Startled, Rose replied, "What do you mean?"

"What do you think about when you think about a non-smoker?" it continued.

"Well," she said, "I suppose I think about smoke."

"Precisely. So what did you bring to yourself?"

"Smoke," she replied, surprised at her answer.

"You created exactly what you were holding in your mind," said the voice.

"Then how do I manifest what I want?" Rose asked.

"What do you dislike about smoking?" the voice queried.

She thought for a moment and answered, "It smells bad, when you kiss the guy he tastes bad, and it's generally unhealthy."

"So," continued the voice, "what do you want *instead* of those things?"

Suddenly, she understood! Laughing, she replied, "I want someone who smells good, tastes good and is healthy!"

Having made this revelation, she was finally able to create it. To my knowledge, she is still with the man she met soon thereafter – a man who did not smoke. I cannot vouch for his smell or taste, but they certainly make a good couple, because Rose (after clarifying the non-smoker issue) also clarified the rest of her list. She created precisely what she desired because she was clear about what she wanted.

All too often, we are clear about the things we do not desire, focusing on our dislike of those negative qualities or experiences. Remember the Universal Law of Energy that "like attracts like"? What we hold in our minds, we create. Just like Rose, we will draw exactly what we envision, so the clarity of our vision is of paramount importance.

The next exercise is one of the central pillars of the work outlined in this book. This is what I call a *Magic Wand Exercise*. In a humorous turn of events, the first time I typed this chapter, I repeatedly mistyped the word "wand" and instead typed "want." Since there are no accidents, you can also look at this as a Magic *Want* Exercise since you are clarifying what you want to create in your life. Before you begin, take out the list from the earlier exercise detailing where and how you are being drained in your life and where you are being an emotional sponge. Use these observations to help you with this *Magic Wand/Want Exercise*.

Here we go.

*****

Exercise

MAGIC WAND/WANT, PART 1

I hand you a magic wand to create your magic wants. I say to you, "Here is a magic wand. You may wave it once, and create the perfect life for yourself. What do you want in that perfect life? What qualities, experiences or things?"

Take out a piece of paper and make two columns. To the left, title the column, "What I Want." To the right, title the column "What I Do Not Want."

Remember Rose? In order to get to the heart of her true desires, she had to first define those things that were not harmonious to her vision of perfection. To begin, then, think about those things (qualities, experiences, energies or things) which you dislike and do not desire to re-create in your new, perfect life and put them in the right hand column. That column may also include many of the things from your earlier drainage/sponge lists.
*In the column to the left, put those things that you **do** desire.*

The lists may be as short or long as necessary.

*****

The following is an example of a list created by one of my clients, whom I will call Anne:

WHAT I WANT	WHAT I DO NOT WANT
Happiness	My career dominating my life
Peace of mind	Being drained by my clients
Good health	Too many demands at work
Wealth	Conflict
A hassle-free, chaos-free home	Confusion
Stability for my children	Dealing with big egos
To follow my spiritual path	Not enough money
More time with my husband	Lack of clarity and vision
More freedom	Having people take advan tage of me
Time alone	
Honesty	
I need a new job!	

*****

Exercise

MAGIC WAND/WANT, PART 2

Now, having finished your lists, take a good look at the "don't want" list. Examine each thing on the list and ask yourself these questions: What do I want instead of this? What is the positive opposite of this thing? Once defined, place the new item on the list to the left.

Once that "don't want" list is empty, move on to the left. Examine where you have repeated yourself by listing the same item in different ways. This will shorten your list slightly.

*****

After she made her list, Anne and I sat down to eliminate the negatives on it. Some of the items were simple to switch. Whenever you see phrases like "lack of" or "not enough of" you can simply remove those words and switch the positive concept over. For instance, "lack of clarity and vision" becomes "clarity and vision" and "not enough money" simply becomes "money." Examine your list for those types of phrases, since they are the simplest to eliminate.

Often you will find concepts that are tied to one another. On this list, "my career dominating my life" and "too many demands at work" are closely connected. Although they are not the same specific issues, both deal with an overabundance of energy directed at work, leaving Anne with less energy to deal with the rest of her life.

"Talk to me about your job," I said to Anne.

"Yikes! Where do I start?" she asked.

I thought for a moment. "Well, it seems as though many things on this list relate to work. What is the issue of work dominating your life?"

Anne jumped right in. "I spend far more than forty hours every week dealing with work. I constantly have to bring work home. Whenever I delegate, it seems that I have to go behind the people and fix their messes. Also, they've downsized my company and I'm doing the work of several people, not just one. I rarely get time to breathe, much less eat lunch or take breaks or anything. And the people I see, my clients, are constantly needy and drain my energy."

"Whew! That sounds exhausting," I replied. "So let's get underneath it a little. Remember that we're at the point of eliminating the negative concepts, replacing them with positive ones. So, rather than the massive amounts of extra work and the work of several people, what would you prefer?"

"Frankly," she laughed, "I'd prefer another job. In lieu of that, however, I suppose my preference would be to have manageable deadlines and more help."

I perused her original list. "Looking here, I see an item which says 'a hassle-free, chaos-free home.' How about a 'hassle-free, chaos-free work environment'?"

"Great!" she exclaimed.

"Now, before we add that to the list, let's look at the terms 'hassle-free' and 'chaos-free.' In both, the important concepts are negative. You must negate 'hassle' and 'chaos.'"

"Oh," Anne thought. "OK. Effortless?"

"Nope," I smiled. "Here again, the important concept is

'effort.' How about 'harmonious'? And what about 'efficient'?"

Anne thought for a moment and resolved, "OK. Let's change them to 'harmonious and efficient.'"

"Done," I replied.

Through similar conversation, constantly asking, "If this is something you don't want, then what would you prefer?," we eliminated a number of other items. The issue of the dominating career became "balance." Her problems with being drained by her clients became "energizing relationships." The big ego issue and the problem with people taking advantage of her became "mutually-respectful relationships." The extremely common issue of "not enough money" became "financial abundance."

Anne's list transitioned into:

WHAT I WANT	WHAT I DO NOT WANT
Happiness	Conflict
Peace of mind	Confusion
Good health	
Wealth	
A harmonious and efficient home	
Stability for my children	
To follow my spiritual path	
More time with my husband	
More freedom	
Time alone	
Honesty	
I need a new job!	
Clarity	
Vision	
A harmonious and efficient workplace	
Energizing relationships	
Mutually-respectful relationships	
Financial abundance	

What remained on her "don't want" list were two single words, "conflict" and "confusion." Many times, your list will include single words like these. I call these "catch words." They tend to be rather ambiguous. Before asking yourself what you would prefer, first ask the question, "How do I define this term?"

Anne defined "conflict" as "anger, shouting, judgement,

people not listening to each other, everyone assuming they are right and everyone else is wrong." With this definition in mind, I asked her what she would prefer. First, we realized that the addition of "mutually-respectful relationships" dealt with a great deal of the conflict issues. Second, we added the term "peace," a word that felt like the opposite of "conflict" to Anne.

To eliminate "confusion" we applied the same process of first defining the term and then determining the opposite of it. For Anne, "confusion" meant, "chaos, lack of focus." Her list already included "clarity" to negate the lack of focus. We added the terms "stability" and "groundedness" to create the opposite of "chaos."

Anne further refined her list as follows:

WHAT I WANT   WHAT I DO NOT WANT

Happiness
Peace of mind
Good health
Wealth
A harmonious and efficient home
Stability for my children
To follow my spiritual path
More time with my husband
More freedom
Time alone
Honesty
I need a new job!
Clarity
Vision
A harmonious and efficient workplace
Balance
Energizing relationships
Mutually-respectful relationships
Financial abundance
Peace
Stability
Groundedness

The final simple step before moving on is to see where you have repeated yourself. This will shorten the list slightly. In the list above, you see "financial abundance" and "wealth." Also, "peace" and "peace of mind" as well as "stability" and "stability for my children." In all these cases, pick the one that better encompasses both. Anne crossed off "wealth," "peace of mind" and "stability for my children," since the other concepts were more expansive and inclusive. Finally, we combined two items into one, creating the phrase "mutually-respectful, energizing relationships."

Below, you will see how Anne's list continued the process of transformation. Keep this list handy, since I will refer back to it in the next chapter:

WHAT I WANT	WHAT I DO NOT WANT
Happiness	
Good health	
A harmonious and efficient home	
To follow my spiritual path	
More time with my husband	
More freedom	
Time alone	
Honesty	
I need a new job!	
Clarity	
Vision	
A harmonious and efficient job	
Balance	
Mutually-respectful, energizing relationships	
Financial abundance	
Peace	
Stability	
Groundedness	

Take a moment to review your list and finalize it utilizing the techniques discussed above. Once you have completed this task, your first major step is done. You have your list. What is next?

You've got to accentuate the positive,
Eliminate the negative,
Latch on to the affirmative,
Don't mess with Mister-In-Between.[8]

—Johnny Mercer/Harold Arlen, from the song "Accentuate The Positive"

Chapter 6

Accentuate The Positive

The process of creating desired results in your life begins with clarity. In the previous chapter, you learned to define what you want much more clearly. But this clarification is not enough to ensure the desired results. You must also dig beneath the surface and discern *why* you want each of the things on your list.

My client Larry provided a major learning experience for me on the importance of asking, "why." When I first began to work with the issues of manifestation and protection, Larry came to me for spiritual coaching, having reached a crisis point in his marriage. Although many things came up, one of his primary issues was around money. When Larry made his "Magic Wand/Want" list, one of the most important considerations in his conception of a perfect life was making more money. Originally, his list said, "I do not want to struggle financially." As you recall from the last chapter, in order to manifest, it was necessary for him to turn that around. For Larry, the positive opposite of "financial struggle" was "abundant finances."

After some time, Larry's finances still had not improved. If anything, they were worse, and his marriage was shakier than before. Returning to me, Larry asked me to help him figure out why he could not seem to achieve his desired goal of financial abundance when his intention was so focused. In a moment of startling clarity, I saw the root of the problem.

I asked Larry, "Why do you want financial abundance?"

"That's simple," he said. "I want more money so that I don't have to struggle."

"That is a circular answer, Larry," I said. "What are the things that more money will give you that you do not have now?"

After thinking for a moment, he replied, "Less stress around paying the bills, nicer things like better clothes and a nicer car. More freedom to do what I want. Also, being able to buy nice things for my wife and kids when they want them."

I finally started to get it! "OK," I said. "Why do you want less stress around paying the bills?"

Larry looked at me as if I were stupid and answered, "That's a stupid question. Nobody wants stress."

Unperturbed (mostly), I asked, "If that's true, then why no stress? What do you want instead?"

"Oh, I see what you're getting at," Larry said. "I want peace and tranquility." He looked a bit smug at having answered so readily.

I smiled. "Why?"

"What do you mean?" he asked.

"Why do you want peace and tranquility? What's so great about them?"

Larry looked confused, but thought a moment and said, "They make me feel happy, comfortable."

"Great!" I shouted. "So, Larry, what do you *really* want?"

"Happiness?" he asked.

"Yes. For one thing. So let's move on. The other things you said money would provide were about buying things for yourself, your wife and your kids. Why?"

He was finally getting more interested. "Well, buying those kinds of things makes me feel happy and comfortable. Successful."

"Successful by whose definition?" I asked.

"Success is success. If you make a lot of money, you are successful."

"Even if you are happy and content with less money," I asked. Larry pondered that and finally conceded, "No. You are right. If you are happy, then I suppose you are successful."

"So," I asked, "whose definition of success equals more money?"

After much more discussion, we uncovered the root of the issue. Larry's wife had extremely expensive tastes. She was constantly talking to him about the need to make more money. As a result, Larry was living out his wife's desire for more success, which to her meant more money. In reality, Larry wanted happiness and tranquility. What stood in the way of that was not money, but the disparity between his perceived desires (drawn from his wife) and his true desires. For Larry, the issue of money was not the true issue. He thought he wanted money, but when we uncovered the "why?" behind it, we discovered that what he really wanted was a better relationship with his wife. Money, though potentially a short-term solution, was not the core of the lack in his life. Asking that simple question, "why?" expanded and clarified things in a way I had never before experienced in my life or my practice.

Taking Larry's lesson to heart, let us revisit your *Magic Wand/ Want* list. Now that you have created the list and reduced it by eliminating the duplications, you are ready to discover what you really want, and why you want it!

*****

Exercise

ASKING "WHY?," PART 1

Take your list of what you want to create the perfect life for you and, for each item on the list, ask yourself, "Why do I want this? What will this give me? Why is this on my list?"

*****

For an example, we will return to our friend Anne. After the first round of *Magic Wand/Want Exercises*, Anne's list looked like this:

WHAT I WANT   WHAT I DO NOT WANT

Happiness
Good health
A harmonious and efficient home
To follow my spiritual path
More time with my husband
More freedom
Time alone
Honesty
I need a new job!
Clarity
Vision
A harmonious and efficient job
Balance
Mutually-respectful, energizing relationships
Financial abundance
Peace
Stability
Groundedness

Like Larry in the example above, I asked Anne, "Why do you want financial abundance?" Ultimately, for Anne at least, the issue was one of freedom. With more money, she felt she would have more freedom in her life. The phrase "more freedom" already appears on the list. As a result, we erased the specific concept of money and permitted the broader, more inclusive concept of freedom to encompass the more focused issue of money. In a similar fashion, we can collapse a number of other items on the list into this powerful concept of "freedom." The concept of "good health" for Anne was about having the physical and emotional strength to be able to do whatever she desired to do. A perfect definition of "freedom"! Not only that, but the ideas of time to follow her spiritual path and more time with her husband were all encapsulated for Anne in the inclusive concept of "freedom."

In addition, Anne noted a few duplications on the list. "Happiness," "peace," "stability" and "groundedness" all fell into the concept of feeling more empowered and spiritually self-aware. Thus, we eliminated all of those words and replaced them with "empowerment" and "self-knowledge."

Her list modified into:

WHAT I WANT	WHAT I DO NOT WANT
A harmonious and efficient home	
Freedom	
Time alone	
Honesty	
I need a new job!	
Clarity	
Vision	
A harmonious and efficient job	
Balance	
Mutually-respectful, energizing relationships	
Empowerment	
Self-Knowledge	

One phrase on her list which particularly caught my attention was, "I need a new job!" What about this word "need"?

NEED: *Something essential to survival.*

Using that definition, what must we have in order to survive? Air, food, water and shelter. Those are the only requirements for basic human survival. All other issues, items and ideas fall under the heading of *preferences*. We need air and water, but we might prefer clean rather than polluted. We need food, but we might prefer specific types of food, cooked rather than raw, or vegetables instead of meat. We need shelter, but we might prefer a specific kind of shelter, a house rather than a lean-to, perhaps. You get the idea.

When we attach the word *need* to any concept, we immediately create the energy that we cannot survive without that thing. For Anne to say she needs a new job creates the energy that she cannot function without it, which her very survival depends on this item. When something feels essential, it is not a basic, survival need, but rather a need *in order to*. By this I mean that we often need one thing in order to create another. When you have a goal or vision that requires something else to catalyze its creation, you then *need* that catalyst *in order to* create the goal. If your goal is to pay off a $2,000 credit card debt, then you need that money in order to manifest that vision. The money itself is not a basic survival need, but it is a necessary component of the creation of the desired result.

With this perspective of *need* vs. *need in order to*, re-examine Anne's list, beginning with the phrase, "I need a new job." First, when Anne and I revisited this list, we changed it to read, "I want a new job." Next, I asked the infamous question, "Why?"

Anne sighed, "Here we go again. OK. Why do I *want* a new job? We've been over this already. It drains me."

"Do you enjoy the nature of what you do?"

"Oh, yes," Anne replied brightly. "As you know, I work in social services, and I love the feeling of being able to help people."

"So it's not your career that bothers you so much, it's the energy of the workplace?" I asked.

"Definitely," she averred. "I've always loved what I do. Before the downsizing, I even loved working in my current office."

"In that case," I continued, "what you are really asking for is a different working environment. Already on your list is 'harmonious and efficient workplace' as well as clear definitions of the type of relationships you prefer, correct?"

"Yes," she replied.

"Do you feel comfortable eliminating this phrase 'I need a new job' and letting the other issues stand it its place?"

She thought for a moment, looked at the list and said, "You know, you're right. I've said pretty clearly what I want here, so this is redundant. Let's take if off!"

By doing away with the concept of need, Anne was able to focus much more clearly on the core of what she truly desired. This is an example of the total elimination of the word "need" from the list. As discussed earlier, however, "need" can often be replaced with "need in order to."

Also on Anne's list, we found the phrase, "Time alone." When I asked her about this, she replied, "I really need that." Here is that word again! We discovered that her need was actually a "need in order to." In this case, Anne needed the time alone in order to finish a training manual she had been asked to write. Without the occasional isolation, she was unable to clarify and focus. Thus, we replaced the phrase "time alone" with "clarity" and "focus." Both of these concepts were extremely important to Anne, who frequently worked with deadlines and the communication of information that had to be precisely and clearly presented. In addition, they replaced the specific idea of "vision" on her list.

Thus, Anne's list changed as follows:

WHAT I WANT	WHAT I DO NOT WANT
A harmonious and efficient home	
Freedom	
Honesty	
Clarity	
A harmonious and efficient job	
Balance	
Mutually-respectful, energizing relationships	
Empowerment	
Self-Knowledge	
Focus	

*****

Exercise

ASKING "WHY?," PART 2

Examine your needs. Continue the exercise by examining where you have used the word "need" on your list.

First, see where you may have already replaced this concept with more empowering terms. Ask yourself, "Why do I feel I need this? What would it give me?"

If these questions do not help, then change the "need" into "need in order to" and then fill in that blank.

For instance, if your list says, "I need a new house" change that to read, "I need a new house in order to _____."

Once you have done this, ask yourself, "Why do I desire the item or items in the blank? What will this give me?"

*****

Occasionally, something on the list will not fit well into the questions "Why do I want this? What will this give me?" In this case, you might want to ask yourself, "How do I define this?" Back to Anne for an example. You will see on her list the word, "honesty."

I asked Anne, "What do you mean by 'honesty'?"

Anne looked puzzled and said, "Everyone knows what honesty is."

"Suppose I were to walk up to you and notice that you have spinach in your front teeth. I point it out to you in public, causing many people to turn and look? How would that make you feel?"

"Not so great," she said.

"Now. Suppose I walk up to you, take you aside quietly and tell you that you have spinach in your teeth and you might want to do something about it before you embarrass yourself? How would that make you feel?"

"That's much nicer," she said.

"They're both honest," I told her. "Which would you prefer?"

"The second one, of course."

"But you say you want honesty, so either one fulfills the request. What you really want is not just 'honesty,' but a certain style of communication, a certain quality."

"That's right. What I want is for people to communicate with me openly, with compassion."

Once again, the phrase "mutually respectful relationships" popped up as the deeper issue underneath the term "honesty." The energy of such relationships also made Anne reconsider the specific listing of the harmonious and efficient home and workplace. For Anne, mutually respectful relationships would cultivate harmony and efficiency. They would also fill her desire for sharing and mutual growth. As a result of these revelations, we deleted "harmonious and efficient workplace" and "harmonious and efficient home," allowing "mutually respectful relationships" to take their place. We also added the specific concepts of "mutual sharing" and "growth" which had suddenly come up for Anne as an important issue that had not yet been addressed on the list.

Her list shortened and became more focused on the true, core issues which, for Anne, were vital components of the perfect life. As an example, here is the next version of Anne's list.

<u>WHAT I WANT</u>	<u>WHAT I DO NOT WANT</u>
Freedom	
Clarity	
Balance	
Empowerment	
Self-Knowledge	
Mutually-respectful, energizing relationships	
Mutual sharing	
Growth	

*****

Exercise

ASKING "WHY?," PART 3

So, let us return to your list. Finish the exercise by asking "How do I define this?" for each of the items which were not covered under parts 1 or 2 of this exercise.

*****

Examine your list. Make sure that everything clearly expresses your desires and goals. Before moving on, I ask that you place one thing back on your list. In the (now empty) "What I Do

Not Want" column, place two items.

The first is the word "negativity." Recall our working definition of the word, "Energy that is intentionally designed to cause harm." The second is the phrase, "All things that intentionally block me from manifesting what I desire." You have clarified what you want and now must make sure that you encompass anything intentionally harmful that you may have forgotten as well as anything that intentionally blocks you from achieving your goals.

Anne's final list looked like this:

WHAT I WANT	WHAT I DO NOT WANT
Freedom	Negativity
Clarity	All things that intentionally block me
Balance	from manifesting what I desire
Empowerment	
Self-Knowledge	
Mutually-respectful, energizing relationships	
Mutual sharing	
Growth	

At this point in the process, Anne asked me a fascinating question. She said, "I thought we were working on how to shield things away from me. Why all this work on clarifying the things I want?"

The answer is this: At least ninety percent of protecting your energy must be about drawing to you what you desire. Remember Rose and the story about the non-smoker? When you focus on what you wish to push away or repel, you run the risk of bringing it closer to you. When I asked several friends to share with me how they shielded themselves, my friend Danielle provided a wonderful description to help illustrate this point. In her words:

"I guess what I do could be considered shielding myself against negative psychic energy, but I don't think of it as protecting myself so much as *opening* myself. My approach to difficult people and situations is to respond with love–consciously sending out loving thoughts, feelings and energy. The way I feel it works for me is that it opens me to loving possibilities, probably blocking any incompatible energy that might be coming my way, and results in a peaceful flow for me on physical, emotional, mental and spiritual levels.

"If I'm around somebody really gloomy and negative, I send sympathy and compassion with the love, and I may imagine myself surrounded with white light. But mostly, I feel I am sending energy out rather than blocking energy coming in."

Danielle beautifully explores the central paradox of energetic shielding: *how to remain open and closed at the same time.* By focusing on the active sending of energy from herself to others, she remains open. In this way, she consciously directs her energy to become magnetic, rather than obsessing on pushing away those things she does not desire. Since her energy so strongly radiates out what she desires, the energetic flow has little room left for disharmonious things to sneak in, essentially closing her down to that which she does not wish to experience. Rather than moving passively through the world, waiting for things to come to her, she sends out energy to magnetize herself. Both open and closed, she moves through the world with a clear understanding of how she has the power to manifest her own reality.

Having just the vision's no solution,
Everything depends on execution:
Putting it together –
That's what counts.[9]

—Stephen Sondheim, from *Sunday In The Park With George*

Chapter 7

Putting It Together

You have done a great deal of listing and journaling, so now what? This chapter returns you to the cleansing and shielding visualization first learned in Chapter One. This time, however, you have the tools ready to create potent and unique shields designed just for you.

In Chapter One we discussed the idea that energy just "is." It has neither positive nor negative polarity, and moves through intention. The visualizations at the end of that chapter helped you create potent, yet nonspecific, shields. The bubble of iridescent energy with which you surrounded yourself received very broad instructions. Now, however, you have much more specific instructions to give.

Before going on to the visualization below, take out the final copy of your *Magic Wand/Want List* and familiarize yourself with it. If you memorize the list, then the visualization can be done with your eyes closed. If not, when the time comes to read the list aloud, simply have it available in your lap or next to your chair so that you can open your eyes and read it easily. When you are done, close your eyes and complete the exercise.

SPECIFIC CLEANSING AND PROTECTION

Settle into a comfortable position. Close your eyes and begin slowly breathing in through your nose and out through your mouth. Take a nice deep breath in, and release. Allow yourself to focus in on your breathing.

Each time you inhale, feel yourself fill with energy. As you exhale, allow yourself to sink deeper and deeper into comfort. Allow the tension and thoughts of the day to simply float away out of your mind with each exhalation.

In your mind's eye, envision yourself in your sacred space. Take a moment to see the sights around you: the beauty of nature, the sky, any plants or animals that happen to be there. Smell the aroma of the growing plants and flowers. If you are near the ocean, smell the salt air. Feel the warmth of the sun on your face and body. A gentle breeze lightly caresses you as it flows by. You can almost taste the pristine, pure air. As you focus around you, you can also hear the light play of the breeze, the sound of birds. Everything is beautiful and clean.

As you stand in this beautiful place, envision yourself being showered in energy. It is coming from above you and it gently flows down, flows over your head, flows down your body. You feel yourself bathed in this beautiful energy.
As the energy flows down you, you feel all of the tension melting out of your body. As you look at yourself, you begin to see the toxins releasing. All of the external and internal things that have stuck to you, or stuck in you, are releasing out of you. And the Earth is accepting them as they flow away.

You feel clean and pure and lighter than you have ever

felt before, as all of these things simply flow off you, flow out of you and release. Allow yourself to bathe in this beautiful, warm energy as it continues to gently wash over you and release all things from you that are not harmonious.

Slowly, you feel the energy begin to slow down. It is not flowing as strongly. Now it is just a trickle, for you are as clean as you can be. You feel light and buoyant. You feel alive and vibrant. You feel clean and pure.

In this state, any beings who guide you, the spirit guides, the higher powers, whoever it is, invite them to join you. Welcome them to your space. You will find yourself surrounded in beautiful, loving energy. You are clean, you are pure and you have been joined by beautiful loving beings who support you.

In your mind's eye, envision yourself surrounded by a bubble of iridescent, light. You find that, in your lightness, you have raised off of the ground and you are floating a few inches above the Earth. The bubble of energy surrounds you on all sides, above and below. You are encased in a beautiful bubble of sparkling, iridescent energy.

At this time, bring into your consciousness your Magic Wand/Want List. Think of each item on this list. Send out your energy and ask that this bubble shield and protect you. Ask that this beautiful bubble surrounding you draw to you only those things on your list, those things you have determined to be harmonious for you at this time in your life. One at a time, focus on each item from the list, feeling as the deep truths begin to imbed themselves into the bubble, becoming one with your energy.

Now, ask that the bubble also bring to you all of those things that are for your highest and best good. Next, ask that any energies which will not support you and help you be reflected away with love. Ask that any of these beings who have joined you will help you to maintain this beautiful bubble of energy. They will add their own energies to it.

As you send this thought out, you see each of these beautiful beings whom you have called to you begin to shimmer and glow. As they begin to shimmer and glow, they lose their form and they become pure light. Their energies slowly approach you and begin to merge into the bubble. Now, it is not just an iridescent bubble, it is sparkling with gold and silver and every color of the rainbow as these pure beings have combined their essence to help shield and protect you.

You feel light and buoyant and vibrant and joyful. You feel yourself tingling as these energies merge. Love and protection surround you. Know that only those things that are harmonious at this time in your life will come to you. Any energy that is intentionally directed at you in order to harm you will be reflected back to the sender with love so that they might learn and grow.

With these joyful thoughts, you begin to feel the bubble of energy moving inward towards you, slowly beginning to encompass you. The energy is touching you now and is conforming to the shape of your body like a second skin. You have internalized this energy of protection. All of this energy of the universe from the beautiful loving beings and from your own intention are merged with you. From now on, you will carry your shields and protection within you at all times. You may expand the energy outward, or you may bring it in as you will, but it is now a part of you and can never be separate. You are one with the energy of the Universe. You are one with the energies of joy and love. You are shielded and protected. You are loved.

Allow yourself to feel your body as you come back down to the ground. As your feet touch the Earth, you begin to feel its energy flowing up through the soles of your feet, slowly beginning to energize you again and bring you back to the room. Your feet begin to tingle. The energy of the Earth travels slowly up your legs to your knees, up your thighs to your hips.

You feel the energy of the Earth begin to travel up your torso to your chest. Your arms come back to life and you slowly begin to feel the energy reaching your face. You can feel the muscles in your face coming back. You feel the energy reach your head and as it swirls through your head, you feel it come to your eyes.

When you are ready, open your eyes and return once again to the room.

*****

You have now programmed your shields to help you manifest your current vision of the "perfect life for you." If there are any areas of that hold more energy for you, you may wish to take what you have learned and narrow the focus a little. Examine your *Magic Want/Want List* to see if there is a primary theme that repeats. Are there several things about friendships, career, marriage or some other area of life? If so, try the following exercise.

*****

Exercise

CLARIFYING SPECIFIC AREAS OF LIFE

Adapt the exercise by asking yourself, "If I had a magic wand and could create the perfect _____ for me, what would it look like?" Fill

*in the blank with one of the following areas or
any other area of your life that draws you:*

> **Career**
> **Intimate Relationship**
> **Health/Body**
> **Friendship with** _____
> **Relationship with my** _____
>   **(mother, father, sister, brother,
>   husband, partner, friend, etc.)**
> **Home**
> **Spiritual path**

*Follow the same steps detailed in the broader
"perfect life" exercise. Use this list to create
shields when you know you are going to experience something relating to the specific area
addressed in the exercise.*

*****

Many clients have had significant results from focusing on specific areas that stood out when they made the initial "perfect life" list. Mark, for example, had a particular issue around the energy of his workplace. As a result, we focused more strongly on the clarification of his "perfect energy in the workplace."

Mark's problems involved staff meetings with hypercritical and unhappy employees who frequently obstructed the process of getting through the agenda. After doing the *Magic Wand/Want Exercise* with the career focus, Mark clarified his boundaries. Before every meeting, he now takes five minutes to cleanse his energy and create specific shields which focus in on his desires around what he wishes to accomplish in the staff meeting. The employees have not appreciably changed their behavior, but Mark's response to them no longer allows the meetings to become a forum for obstructionist argument.

Using these techniques, you can create specific sets of shields for the individual situations in which you find yourself. I create a very different set of shields when I spend time with my family at Thanksgiving than I do when I step in front of a large group to give a lecture. Doing a counseling session requires much different shields than attending a cocktail party. Use your intuition and your common sense to dictate if, when and where you might need to create more targeted and specific shields in your life. In just a few, quiet moments you may be able to eliminate or significantly reduce your stress in previously stressful situations.

When you find yourself in a situation that accelerates suddenly or unexpectedly into an energetic drain, you can train yourself to put up instant, spontaneous shields. Once you have become comfortable with the primary cleansing and shielding exercises, you can draw on that same energy to protect you on a quicker, limited basis. Simply take a deep breath and hold it for a few seconds. Next, slowly exhale and feel yourself physically relaxing as your muscles release. At the same time, envision your boundaries moving outward with the intention of shielding you from the undesirable energy. Practice this technique in a variety of situations until you find a rhythm that works. You may discover that you can perform this exercise easily at meetings, while in conversation with another person, or in any one of many close, public situations without drawing any unwarranted attention to yourself.

Expectations are resentments waiting to happen.[10]

— Anne Lamott, from *Crooked Little Heart*

Chapter 8

Jigsaw Puzzle

Up to this point, you have touched, clarified and focused your energy to create stronger and clearer personal boundaries. However, none of us lives in a vacuum. Once you have done this work, you must then step back out into the world and re-enter the interactive universe of energetic relationships.

Each of us has long-standing relationships with many people, most of whom will have some measure of resistance when we ask them to adapt to our newly created realities. I look at life as a jigsaw, with each person as an individual puzzle piece. We each have a unique shape to the boundaries of our lives, a shape against which all others in our lives learn to fit, thus creating the larger picture of our life out of the individual puzzle pieces.

Once you begin the process of clarifying and altering your personal boundaries, you energetically lift yourself out of the picture of your life and do the work to change the shape of your puzzle piece. You then re-enter the picture, but the other people in our life no longer fit with the new shape you have created. These people have two choices. First, they can adapt and learn to fit with the "new you." Second, they can go away. The "going away" can either be an emotional distance or a literal exit from your life.

Some people will dance a happy dance with you, exulting in the fact that you have finally taken the steps to become happier and more empowered. This group is generally small, but quite vocal in their support.

The next group, those who choose to leave, is usually somewhat larger. When I made the radical shift from working as a theatre director to becoming a minister and spiritual coach, many people left my life in both figurative and literal ways. Some simply became distant and polite, still corresponding but not engaging in the details of my life. Many others actively cut me out of their realities, refusing to answer mail or phone calls.

Both groups of people were unwilling to change their own puzzle pieces to accommodate my new life. To remain close to me, they would have to examine and alter perceptions and beliefs, something they were either unable or unwilling to do. This is not to say that they were "wrong" or "bad" by doing that. They were simply not connected to me strongly enough to make the work of change attractive to them. I often call these people *acquaintances*, rather than *friends*. To be sure, this type of energy causes pain. I was deeply hurt by what I felt to be abandonment by people whom I had considered friends. One of my great lessons, however, was a lesson of balance.

The universe abhors imbalance. Whenever something tips a balance one way, the universe will create something to bring the energy back towards center. Several months after making my radical career transition, I began to notice something odd. Although many people had left my life, I was making an extraordinary amount of new friends. Not only that, but many people from my past, from college or even high school, suddenly began contacting me and re-creating relationships. To replace the energy of those who had left my life, the universe helped to provide me with friends who were now harmonious with my personal energetic path.

The most fascinating group of people, however, are those who truly want to keep you in their life, yet are still resistant to making the personal changes this would require. These people push back against your boundaries, attempting to make you who you were. The people with whom we have the closest relationships often push back the hardest. In Chapter 3, I related the story of my mother and how I allowed her to use me for many years as both an "energy sundae" and an "emotional garbage can." Here is the rest of that story.

As you recall, my mother and I had danced a lifelong co-dependent dance in which I allowed her to drain me so that she might feel better. As I began to create the system outlined in this book, I obviously began to examine all of the relationships in my life. When I looked at my relationship with my mother, I had to laugh. All this time I had been working with clients to help them to stop giving away their energy, only to find a clear example of energy drainage right there in my own life.

On a lovely autumn weekend in 1995, my partner Kevin and I had been invited to spend some time with a friend in the Virginia mountains. Over several days, I had a chance to examine and clarify many issues, among them the co-dependent energetic relationship between my mother and myself. On Saturday, I decided to call her to catch up with the latest family gossip. During the conversation, she began to recount an issue with one of my brothers, something I had heard frequently over a period of time. In the past, I had allowed her to vent, validating her right to be upset, offering vague comfort, and essentially allowing her to unload her anger into me. At the end of these conversations, she always felt better. I, however, felt totally drained.

This particular day, I made what might be termed a "tactical error" in dealing with my mother. As she paused for a breath, I responded, "Well, Mom, why don't we examine why you need to keep this anger? What is it giving you that you are so resistant to let go of?" In essence, I began to treat her like a client. The conversation quickly came to an end.

Two weeks later, my mother had a chance to meet Kevin in person for the first time. After several days, she took him aside and said to him, "You know, I can understand why you would be such a successful spiritual counselor. You are so compassionate and loving. But Tommy is so selfish and egocentric, I can't imagine him helping anyone."

Here was a woman who had always been my greatest fan and advocate, suddenly saying something quite unkind. What was that about? My mother is a generous and loving woman who, to my knowledge, has never intentionally hurt anyone. She clearly wanted this information to get back to me or she would never have spoken to my partner.

I soon realized that she was reacting to my new boundaries, ones that did not allow her to use me as an "energy sundae." My mother was unconsciously pushing back, trying to get me to readjust my boundaries. The "old me" was comfortable to her. The "new me" was no longer available to provide energy or to serve as an emotional garbage can. Because she did not wish to shift her reality, she instinctively pushed back against my new boundaries, attempting to return them to their former place. At that point, I fought a battle within myself between discernment and judgement.

When dealing with people's responses and reactions to you and your boundaries, you must be clear where you are practicing discernment and where you are practicing judgement or self-judgement. Let me give you my working definitions of these terms.

DISCERNMENT: *Knowing what is right or wrong for you.*

JUDGEMENT: *Taking what is right or wrong for you and trying to make it right or wrong for someone else.*

SELF-JUDGEMENT: *Seeing what is right or wrong for someone else and trying to make it right or wrong for you, regardless of your own knowing.*

Right and wrong are not ideas that can be universally applied. As mentioned in the Introduction, I do not believe in a larger, cosmic version of truth for everyone. I do know that each person has his or her personal truth. This personal truth involves the understanding of what works for you and what does not.

RIGHT: *Something that is harmonious with your spiritual path, which helps you feel centered and joyful.*

WRONG: *Anything that does not feel harmonious with your spiritual path, that causes you to feel off-center and unhappy.*

This entire process of creating "invisible armor" involves the development of personal discernment. By clarifying what you want and why you want it, you begin to create a blueprint of what is best for you in any given situation. Once you place that blueprint or template onto someone else, you have moved from discernment into judgement. In their popular play "Inherit The Wind," Jerome Lawrence and Robert E. Lee beautifully encapsulate the concept of judgement. One character says, " . . . one of the peculiar imbecilities of our time is the grid of morality we have placed on human behavior: so that every act of man must be measured against an arbitrary latitude of right and longitude of wrong–in exact minutes, seconds and degrees!"[11]

Judgement generally flows from one of three energies: fear, expectation or assumption. When we do not understand something, we often judge it as wrong, undesirable or worthless. Our society, unfortunately, teaches us to fear that which we cannot understand. Having created this energy around a person or concept, we often lash out against it. My mother's reaction to my clinical detachment, for instance, stemmed from her lack of understanding about my actions which unconsciously translated into a fear that I had pulled away from her. She then lashed out at those actions by lashing out at me.

Another cause of judgemental energy stems from expectation. When we have expectations, by the very nature of the word's definition, we create a mental image of what we want from someone else, but do not communicate that to the other person. In this manner, you will almost always be disappointed. Short of being flawlessly talented mind readers, we can never truly know what someone expects of us unless they tell us.

When the expectations go unfulfilled (as they regularly do), we move into an energy of comparison, resulting in that polarity discussed earlier . . . right/wrong, good/evil, us/them. Your discernment becomes a "grid of morality" against which you measure everyone else in an arbitrary "either/or" system, as in "Either I am right or I am wrong. If I am right, then they are wrong. If I am good, then they are bad." Once you communicate an expectation to someone, it ceases to be an expectation and moves towards becoming an agreement. Until that point, however, expectations foster polarized thinking.

Once you move to polarity thinking, you also begin to make assumptions about other people, another cause of judgemental energy. An "either/or" world leaves little room for individuality of expression. Anything that does not fit into the "right, good" side of things becomes a personal affront. The word "assume" literally means "to take onto oneself." When you are judgemental, you take their energy onto yourself. Certainly, we are all the center of our own universe. We are not, however, the center of anyone else's universe. Few people see critical judgement as the result of towering egotism, but the energies are intimately intertwined. The egotist sees him or herself as the center of everyone's universe. The person who judges others comes from a place of supposing that they have the right answers, the only way.

Self-judgement works in exactly the same manner. We see something that works for another person. We then look at ourselves and attempt to fit into the mold, creating expectations of success. If we do not or cannot conform, we then assume that we are wrong, literally turning the energy inward, taking it into ourselves. It drains us, depletes our personal energy supply and generally makes us feel disempowered.

Whenever you compare yourself with someone else, stop and examine how you feel. Are you simply searching for a frame of reference to understand behavior? If so, then you are fine. If, however, you either judge them or yourself in the process, you are opening your energies up to drainage and depletion.

In working with my clients on issues of judgement, one phrase pops up repeatedly: "There is no such thing as a unilateral relationship." Every energetic interaction, whether conscious or unconscious, involves more than one party. When dealing with other people, we must be particularly clear on this point. Relationships that result in energetic drainage or uncentered feelings almost always result from the actions of more than one person. Although they may occasionally result from the conscious actions of only one person, they will always then depend upon the re-actions of another. Co-dependency requires two participants.

As a result of this realization, I often have to work with clients to get past the desire to blame the other person and begin to take personal responsibility for their participation in the relationship.

Once blame (a judgemental concept) has been noticed, you can begin to replace it with acceptance (a discerning concept). Acceptance does not indicate becoming a doormat. Rather, it points towards an understanding of your own issues so that you can look objectively at the issues of the other person. Often, I ask my clients to step back and try to see things from the perspective of the person whom they wish to blame. At times, I role-play that person for my clients, helping them to understand potential reasons for that person's actions.

So let us return to my mother. My first revelation was of my "tactical error." Rather than gently shift our relationship, I chose to make a sudden, unannounced change. My ownership of the shock of the change helped me to process the anger at her response. The major shift I made was from *judging* her reactions, to *discerning* my co-creation of the situation and then moving to a place of centered detachment in which I "put myself in her shoes." I imagined myself in her place, seeing the confusion I would experience, observing my clinical detachment as coldness and pulling away. My mother's unconscious perception was one of fear; the fear that I had somehow detached from her and no longer wanted the closeness of our prior connection.

I moved from *judging* my mother's reactions into a place of *discerning* how and why she had reacted in such a way. I acknowledged her emotions and realized that she was not consciously trying to hurt me. Rather, she was striving to maintain balance in her own life. I then released my energy. She and I then began a process of give and take, creating more flexible boundaries. Because of our great love for each other, we both compromised somewhat. Now, she often comes to me for advice and counsel. She rarely expects me to listen without expecting me to offer some concrete actions to help her deal with the issues. I no longer serve as an "energy sundae" because she has learned the more nutritious power of actually dealing with issues and resolving them on her own.

Anger and blame at my mother's actions transformed into understanding and acceptance of my co-creation of our relationship. Once I had achieved a more centered perspective, we could begin to rebuild the relationship on new terms. This story of my mother's reactions and our subsequent negotiation illustrates the need for flexibility in your boundaries.

Just as no two people are identical, no two relationships can be identical. There are no cookie-cutter solutions. Your boundaries with a parent will be quite different than those with a sibling. You might allow your best friend to say and do certain things that would infuriate you if they came from a co-worker. The keywords here are flexibility and negotiation. Dialogue with those who hold important positions in your life. Explain your boundaries and determine how to best merge your desires with theirs. Each person has boundary issues. At times, your new boundaries might overstep one of theirs. Avoid judgement, but stay discerning as you negotiate with them to find mutually agreeable middle ground.

Martina, a landscape architect, came to me for spiritual coaching. She had worked for many years developing a spiritual path that included a great deal of Native American energy as well as a healthy dose of Buddhist philosophy. A number of people in her family, however, followed a strict, conservative Christian path. For years Martina had dealt with a great deal of judgemental energy from these people. They were quick to point out how "wrong" she was, but would not listen to her viewpoints.

Over time, Martina developed very clear boundaries around her personal, spiritual truths. She clearly communicated to each of her siblings, basically saying, "Since you won't honor my path, we will no longer discuss it. When we are together we can discuss the family, your children or the weather, but since you won't honor my path by listening to me, I have no interest in discussing it further." Whenever someone began to preach at her, she would either change the conversation or leave the room. For Martina, this boundary helped her maintain a sense of balance, learning the power of centered, defenselessness.

One of her sisters recently approached her and genuinely asked Martina to explain her viewpoints. Her desire to have a relationship with her sister overrode the judgemental patterning with which she had been operating. They have since had some fascinating (and occasionally inflammatory) conversations about religion, spirituality and politics. But they have both remained centered and non-judgemental in the process. With her sister, Martina relaxed what was a firm boundary. This shift of boundary was based on the individual person and their personal energy. She did not eliminate the boundary; she simply adjusted it to fit the unique shape of the new relationship with her sister.

Although Martina chose to develop this expanded relationship with one of her sisters, she did not push the other relationships. One powerful truth Martina embraced was the understanding that we do not have to like or approve of people simply because they are members of our family. In the words of Jacques Delille, "Fate chooses our relatives, we choose our friends."[12] Martina continued to love her family, but came to peace with the understanding that she did not particularly like many of them and certainly did not like or enjoy their actions.

I once asked her, "If you could choose whether or not to have a relationship with each member of your family, which ones would you choose as friends?" She thought for a while and responded, "Only one or two of them!" She began to understand the difference between "like" and "love" and released a great deal of repressed energy. First, she released the frustration at not being able to, in her words, "get them to understand me." Second, she released her guilt at feeling so detached from most of her biological family. Finally, she embraced the concept that we *choose* our true family, those people with whom we desire to share the details of our lives.

For those people with whom you desire to share your life, and those with whom you frequently find yourself, try the following exercise.

*****

Exercise

FLEXIBLE BOUNDARIES

Although you will rarely eliminate boundaries, you will often adjust them individually for each person. Examine each of the items on your Magic Wand/Want List in conjunction with each major person in your life. For each person, look independently at each item

and think about how you might wish to create that particular boundary with that person. You may wish to journal on this assignment.

*****

Before we move on, we must touch on a few potential difficulties that may await you after clarifying your boundaries. Once you have done the work to adjust your personal reality–to change the shape of your puzzle piece–you have two potential, judgemental behavior patterns that could emerge. I call them *over-enthusiasm* and *sanctimony*.

OVER-ENTHUSIASM

Imagine winning a $200 million lottery. You boundless enthusiasm propels you to tell everyone you know, to share your joy with them. Stepping onto a path of greater joy and empowerment can be very much like winning a lottery. You become incredibly enthusiastic. In this enthusiasm, you begin to share your story with others. This sharing of joy is a wonderful and natural process. Unless you are careful, however, you run the risk of becoming *over-enthusiastic*. In this state, you keep trying to convince people that they must try whatever has helped you. Even when they express disinterest, you keep pushing. After a period of time, people can become resentful of your persistence.

Jill came to me for spiritual coaching after going through a particularly painful divorce. Over the course of several months, we worked to help her take back her sense of self-esteem and to create better boundaries in all areas of her life. After some time, she got a better job, lost weight and began dating a wonderful man. An interesting issue popped up during the middle of all this work. Up to the point of her divorce, she had had fairly good relationships with her sisters. After working on her spiritual path for a while, these relationships began to deteriorate. Was it jealousy about her new boyfriend? Her new job? Her weight loss? We could not quite determine the cause of the problems.

After some time, however, I slowly began to perceive a

pattern. Jill had such phenomenal results that she desired to share them with her family. She kept giving her sisters my card, buying them spiritual books, talking to them about her success and how she knew it could help them. Both of her sisters expressed polite interest at first, but were clearly not prepared to embrace the path that Jill had embraced. Her persistence turned the polite interest into resentment. They began to dread talking to Jill because they knew she would bring it up again. They avoided her, stopped returning her calls and basically shunned her at family functions.

Jill was crestfallen after one such gathering. I was finally able to clearly identify the problem and share it with her. In her enthusiasm, she became pushy. I remember clearly saying to her, "Share you joy, share your story, offer them information, but allow them to come to you when and if they are ready." Jill took this to heart and has since begun to rebuild her relationship with her sisters.

The message here is to share your path without any expectations or assumptions. Recall the earlier discussion of judgement? When you do not honor the personal path of another person, you are judging them as being wrong. Discernment will tell you that your path is perfect for you, just as their path (no matter how it appears to be) is perfect for them at the time. When they are ready to embrace a new reality, they will reach out for it, often seeking your advice.

Your quickest way to help someone embrace a more fulfilling path is to role model that path through your words and actions. By simply living a more empowered life, Jill began to notice a shift in the energy of both her sisters. One by one, they started asking her more "spiritual" questions, allowing her to share her insights and experiences. Jill learned to channel her enthusiasm into the daily experiences of her life without feeling the need to push her joy at other people. Rather, she learned to share the joy, offering it as an example without expectation of the response.

SANCTIMONY

A more active and insidious form of this judgemental energy results in sanctimonious behavior. Here, the spiritual seeker begins to feel that they are more evolved, more empowered or more connected than someone else. This feeling creates a hierarchical, polar energy of "greater than vs. less than" or "right vs. wrong." Having reached a point of great clarity in your own life, you must be careful that you do not then presume that you are suddenly somehow better than anyone else is.

> **SANCTIMONY**: *Judgemental assumption that what is right or wrong for you is the only truth and all other truths are less valid.*

Each one of us has a unique, personal spiritual path through which we play out the individual energy of our soul–our connection to the Divine. No single person has "the way" or "the truth" for everyone, because there is no greater way or truth that fits everyone equally. Once you begin to assume the energy of thinking you know what is best for another person, you essentially place yourself on a pedestal, inviting others to bow at your altar.

Darlene was an acquaintance of our friend Jim. One day, she phoned him.

"I've left my husband and moved to Colorado," she told him.

Stunned, Jim asked, "Why? You seemed so happy."

"Well, I just decided that he was not spiritual enough for me. After taking that last light body class, I realized that I was on a higher spiritual path and he was just not evolved."

Jim was still taken aback. "Did he give you grief about your spiritual work?" he asked.

"Not at all. But he just was not willing to learn any of the things which are important."

Jim replied, "So, what you're telling me is that he supported you, provided money for you to take the trainings and classes, never said you were wrong and never stood in your way. Is that about it?"

Darlene answered, "He did that, but he's just not as spiritual as me." And that was the end of the conversation as far as Darlene was concerned.

Be very careful that once you redefine your boundaries, you do not actively push people away because they do not share your new beliefs. If someone supports you and allows you to follow your path without judging you, then they are harmonious with your path regardless of their personal belief systems. Most of us would vehemently deny that we have the energy of sanctimony. To be certain, however, ask yourself the following questions:

> *When you are with a group of people who share your spiritual beliefs, do you talk about other people, discussing how sorry you feel for them that they are not aware? That they just don't understand? That they would only be happy if they would just do what you have done, or learn what you have learned?*

> *Do you dismiss other spiritual belief systems that you find judgemental or limiting?*

> *When discussing your spiritual beliefs with someone who has different beliefs, have you ever simply ended the conversation by saying, "You just don't understand"?*

If you answered "yes" to any of the above questions, then you have flirted with the energy of sanctimony. No matter how much you feel that someone's path does not work well for him or her, you must release your judgement and allow them to follow what they feel, just as you would like them to allow you the same. Recall the Second Universal Law of Energy, "What you send out comes back to you." If you send out sanctimony, then you will receive it back, usually in the form of judgement.

One of the ways in which we draw this energy to us is through unresolved anger. Throughout our lives, people have said and done things that created anger, frustration, irritation or bitterness in us. All too often, we internalize these feelings, carrying them with us for years or even decades. These energies reside within us, subtly yet powerfully keeping themselves alive. They alter our perceptions and actions in order to magnetize identical energy to themselves, feeding the old disempowering emotions.

How can you uncover these subtle forces? The following is one of my favorite exercises, one to help you discover those people who still bring up unresolved energy in your life. This exercise is best done out loud. You can do it alone, or have a close friend assist you.

If you choose to have an assistant, make completely sure you are comfortable saying anything in front of them. Most importantly, make sure they are not on your list!

*****

Exercise

NYAH, NYAH!

Begin by reviewing your life in five-year increments. Think about any major events or people in each section. Who were the authority figures, parents, grandparents, teachers, friends, parents of friends or other people who you encountered in those years?

As you think about these people, do any of your remembrances bring up energy? Do you have a surge of adrenaline? Anger? Rage? Irritation? Do you recall any specific conversations or incidents?

Write down the name of each person who brought up energy for you. Next, examine your list of desires. Envision yourself achieving everything on your "What I Want" list, creating a perfect life of joy and happiness. You are ready to begin.

Beginning with the first person on your list, imagine the following scenario:

You see that person and approach them. Your life is perfect. Everything they said or did to make you feel small, wrong, insignificant or otherwise disempowered has no place in your reality now. You step up to them and rub their face in it!

You heard me correctly. Let 'em have it! Just like a

petulant child, say to them, "Nyah, nyah! My life is perfect and yours isn't. Ha, ha!"

Say everything you have always wanted to say without editing yourself. Forget about propriety, spirituality, right, wrong, good, bad or any of that other critical garbage. Curse, rail, scream, shout, call them rotten names, invoke the most scurvy of curses down onto their heads. No matter how vile or unevolved your critical mind wants to say your words are, keep at it. Don't edit yourself. Imagine what you would like to do as well, any actions you want to take in conjunction with your words. Go for it! Let you imagination run wild.

Continue this exercise for each person on your list until you have either exhausted yourself or the list (or both).

Now take a deep breath. Do you feel better? It's a little like lancing a painful boil. Once the pus has drained out you feel ever so much better. And now the true healing can begin.

Revisit the people on your list one by one. For each one say a three-part prayer of forgiveness. First, forgive yourself for what you just said. Second, forgive them for whatever you perceive as their actions against you. Finally, forgive yourself for your co-creation of that disempowering relationship.

Once you have finished this process, go back once again. Examine each person again and see if you still have any energy. Invariably, some of the names can be crossed off the list and released. Conversely, some names will remain. These people are ones with whom you may have deeper, layered issues that may require more intensive work before you can clarify and release them.

When I first began to examine these issues, I did the *Nyah Nyah Exercise.* One surprising face popped up to me: my second-grade school teacher! When I thought of her, I recalled a specific event. One day we were doing an artistic project. At some point during the day, she looked at my work and criticized it. My only recollection was being upset and angry and thinking, "I can't draw."

To this day, were you to ask me, "Are you an artist?" my first response would almost surely be, "No. I can't draw." Throughout my life, this subtle anger and feeling of disempowerment embedded itself into my subconscious, persistently validating itself and perpetuating my own belief in my lack of artistic ability. A subtle yet powerful energy within me has kept me for almost thirty years in a state of feeling talentless as a visual artist as these feelings fed themselves–like attracting like. Luckily, through the powerful work of *The Artist's Way* by Julia Cameron, I am well on my way to overcoming this particular block. In fact, I highly recommend that book for anyone who feels blocked in any area of his or her life.

I periodically revisit this exercise to find out where I may have accumulated new baggage, or where something old might have resurfaced. Each time I do it, I find myself laughing out loud at the end. How absurd to hold so much energy, usually about such trivial things, like the minor criticism of my second-grade teacher. And even for those things that are not trivial, the amount of wasted energy is phenomenal. In order to maintain anger (rage, frustration, etc.) you have to use your own energy to contain it and keep it pushed down. That energy could well be used more constructively in your life. The *Nyah Nyah Exercise* often creates a powerful catharsis, a release of pent-up energy very much like a deep, deep sigh. In some cases, my clients have laughingly likened it to the energetic equivalent of throwing up. Not a lovely image to be sure, but quite accurate. You purge the poison to allow space for healing to occur.

Another reason for revisiting this exercise rests in the simple fact that you change. Over time, your perceptions alter and your energies alter with them. As a result, those things from your past, which before held little or no energy, might suddenly loom up as gigantic blocks. On the other hand, things that before were tremendous issues might suddenly appear trivial. By keeping track of these things, you help streamline your processing so as not to waste your time working on issues of little importance. Occasionally revisiting this exercise as well as all of the Magic Wand/Want Exercises keeps you flexible in an ever-changing world.

The point here is flexibility. By avoiding rigidity, you can also avoid judgement and sanctimony. Just as no two people are identical, no two relationships are identical. Like Martina and her sister, your boundaries must shift and flow as you move through the fluid world of changing energy.

As you shift the boundaries of your life, those people with whom you relate shift and change around you. Sometimes they shift with you, other times against you. As you change your boundaries, they often change theirs. Stand firm on the limits of your boundaries, but allow others to work with you to find a comfortable place for both of you to live in harmony with each other. Keep the lines of communication open. Putting your jigsaw puzzle back together can be both joyful and occasionally frustrating, but ultimately is an exhilarating process.

" . . . stop and think about what you are trying to change or fix in your environment and maybe, just maybe, you will decide that it is time to stop COMBING THE MIRROR."[13]

— Kevin Ross Emery, from *Combing The Mirror*

Chapter 9

Combing the Mirror

Many times, the violation of our boundaries comes as a result of our own conscious dropping of those boundaries. We cannot shield ourselves from ourselves. Backsliding need not be an occasion for violent self-recrimination. Many of our strongest, most pervasive patterns may have been with us for decades. Like the well-worn ruts on a dirt road, our tires easily fall into the patterns because they are so ingrained. The old, repressed energies discussed in the previous chapter are some of the most powerful catalysts for backsliding. When you have a potent, unreleased energetic block, that well of energy will continually lead you to actively make choices which highlight the block until you recognize, own and release it.

Once you begin to work with your boundaries, you will invariably find times in which you seem to forget everything you have learned. Whatever you do, please do not give up. Backsliding is a natural part of this process. Even though the exercise is called *Magic Wand*, no such magical tool exists. The restructuring of boundaries requires evolutionary steps and active, daily work. Sometimes the steps are rapid and sometimes they are slow, but they always move in the direction of greater freedom and empowerment.

At times, however, seemingly unproductive energy that clearly defies our preferences gets through to us despite our work. How and why does this occur? If you are still having problems with energetic drainage or absorption, there are at least two potential possibilities why such things occur. First, I will explain the dichotomy between belief and knowing; second, I will discuss how we receive messages from the universe.

> *BELIEF: An idea or concept generated in part by another person and which can be altered as a result of outside influence.*

> *KNOWING: An idea or concept that is an integral part of your reality, one that is not subject to outside influence.*

Let us look at two possible scenarios. First, consider your gender. You are firm in the conviction that you are a certain gender. Were I to walk up to you and try to convince you that you were in reality the opposite gender, you would not budge from your conviction. You know that you have a specific gender. No amount of persuasion could convince you otherwise. Your conviction around your gender is a *knowing*.

Next, consider next your family situation. Suppose you believe yourself to be the biological child of your parents. Were I to walk up to you and try to convince you that you were in reality adopted, I might be able to make a plausible argument. The seeds of doubt would be planted. You might begin to question your prior assumptions. Your conviction around your family situation is a *belief*, an understanding that depends on the influence of outside forces.

With more esoteric concepts, we often hear variations of the idea that "You just have to take it on faith." Some issues of faith become so embedded that they are immovable tenets of our life. The knowing that there is a higher, divine power in the universe provides an excellent example. For many people, this understanding is a belief. They believe in God/Goddess. They could be convinced otherwise. For others, it is a knowing. They absolutely know that there is a God/Goddess and no amount of fast-talk or plausible argument can convince them otherwise.

Many issues of faith, however, are not as easily embedded as the acceptance of a higher power. Nearly all of the items on your *Magic Wand/Want* list come down to issues of faith. You must transition from *believing* you deserve them into *knowing* you deserve them. When an issue (boundless prosperity, happiness, freedom, etc.) exists as a belief rather than a knowing, many things can occur to block the manifestation.

Anne's list included the concept of "freedom." In the reality of her life, she had a little guilt around the idea of creating personal space without her husband. As a result, she came back to me with frustration around her manifestation. Almost everything on her list had begun to coalesce, but she had even less time than before to enjoy those things. Once we uncovered her guilt, we realized that she did not truly know she deserved that extra time, rather she believed it only tentatively. This dichotomy between her words and her energy had created a "hole" in her shielding, allowing all sorts of time-consuming tasks to pile up on her.

Take out your *Magic Wand/Want* list and read each item out loud to yourself. For each one, ask yourself, "How does that make me feel? Did I have any energy when I read that?" If the energy was positive, a feeling of peace or happiness, then you probably have no major discrepancy between belief and knowing around that issue. If any issue brings up a visceral emotional reaction, one of doubt, fear or pain then the odds are good that you have some work to do around feeling deserving of that thing.

The second reason why energy might bypass our shields revolves around messages from the universe. Kevin and I laughingly refer to this process as the "pea shooter" syndrome. In his powerful book, *Combing The Mirror (and other steps in your spiritual path)*, Kevin clearly and humorously explains this concept:

> "At first, when the universe wants you to re-examine your path or direction, it will send a little message which always makes me think of a split pea. Remember when you were a child, those little split peas that you use to shoot through a straw? It's as if someone from a distance shot one and it hit you in the

temple. It's not really painful, just a little annoying. This is when you continue to tell yourself that you will give yourself some meditation time every morning so that you can feel more grounded and healthier about your self and your day. You will take some time for yourself. But every morning, the kids need something, the spouse needs something and you really need to get to work early and finish a project.

"So you get a flat tire, three times in one month, each one delays you for forty-five minutes to an hour. Do you think, 'Gee, the universe might be trying to tell me that the world survived for that time I was unavailable? Maybe I need to take that time so I do not have to manifest those flat tires to give me some time for myself.' Or do you think you are lucky you did not take that extra time or you would have been really late? If this is you, you have just been hit by a split pea.

"If you still ignore what you need to do, then you get the marble thrown at your back. The very next week you have a fourth flat tire, but this time you try to change it yourself (the tow truck takes too long) and you throw your back out and are laid up for a couple of days. Flat on your back, bed rest. Now, are you re-examining your priorities or are you lying there trying to figure how you can catch up? If you are figuring how to catch up, the universe has a present for you!

"Baseball anyone? Upside your head at close range. Now you are driving too fast, running late, because you have overcommitted yourself and you have an accident that lands you in the hospital for several days and the car is totaled. You spend all your time figuring out how you are going to catch up. So you decide to go against doctor's orders and go back to work early.

"You're up and your next sport is bowling with a bowling ball knocking you off your feet. You go back to work to early, complicate the situation and end up back in the hospital for six weeks. And if you are still in denial about the need to make some life changes, then you get what I call the big wake-up call.

"The big wake-up call is when you open up the door one morning to find you are trapped in the doorway and a New York wrecking ball is headed directly for you. This could be anything from diagnosis of a terminal illness to a heart attack. Maybe your partner (who you thought was happy) walks out on you. Whatever it is that hits you, it is a life-changing or life-shattering event. It is the kind that makes you cry, 'Uncle!' "[14]

This is not to imply an angry or vengeful God/Goddess energy. On the contrary, these messages begin as a gentle prodding–subtle information designed to keep us moving on a path that is perfectly right for us. Once we ignore the gentler messages, however, those powers within and around us which serve as guides and protectors must "turn up the volume" to get our attention. Your task, then, is to learn how to listen to the "pea shooter" messages in order to avoid meeting that wrecking ball.

Messages come in many forms, but for the sake of discussion I have created six categories: *Coincidence, Dreams, Realizations, Media, Meditation* and *Other People.*

COINCIDENCE

I was once driving outside of San Francisco in very heavy traffic. To keep my mind from obsessing on the poor driving conditions, I decided to think about some of the upcoming business Kevin and I had planned. The one major consideration for the upcoming months was, "Where should we travel next?" Just as I began to ponder this question, a car cut me off in traffic and zoomed out of sight. Strangely, I noticed the license plate was from Colorado.

My first thought was, "Colorado? I have no interest in going there. That can't be the answer to my question." About thirty seconds later, I rounded a curve and saw a billboard advertising a ski vacation in Colorado. At that point, I said to myself, "OK. Maybe that is the answer, but I just don't really know." In less than five minutes, I saw a police car had pulled someone over. Slowing down, I noticed the car, the same Colorado car that had cut me off. Coincidence? Yes, but with a purpose. In fact, Kevin and I did plan business in Colorado and had a very successful trip. This story illustrates an important point. When something catches your attention, particularly something you might categorize as "out of the ordinary," consider the possibility that it might be giving you a message, particularly if you have been pondering a specific question or dealing with an issue. Repetition of the symbol clearly indicates that the Universe wants you to get some point. Learning to pay attention to the seeming coincidences will help you uncover clarity before you have to manifest that wrecking ball.

DREAMS

We all dream every night. Many people have difficulty remembering their dreams, but regardless of that fact, dreams happen for all of us every night. When you have a particularly strong dream, one you recall when you wake up, there could easily be an important message for you imbedded in that dream.

As you progress through the work in this book, it is a good idea to keep your journal next to the bed. If you wake up in the morning with a dream in your memory, grab the journal and jot down whatever you can recall. I do not recommend buying a dream inter- pretation book. Dream interpretation through the analysis of symbols is a very personal issue, unique for each dreamer. No two people will have the exact same correspondence for a specific symbol. Certain guidelines, however, might help you unravel the complexity of your dreams.

First, other people generally represent some aspect of you. When you begin a dream analysis, try interpreting from this perspec- tive first. Ask yourself, "What does the person mean to me? What part of me might they represent." Second, very few symbols have universal meaning, but a few do seem a larger cultural context. The following images often have specific symbolic meaning:

Left side = feminine energy issue
Right side = masculine energy issue
Water = emotions
Weather = the state of emotions
Current home = the present
Old home = the past (whatever period the specific home means to you)
Car = physical body

Try interpreting your dreams with these symbols in mind and see if you begin to perceive any pattern to your dreaming. Are there recurrent symbols? Also, for each dream make sure you note whatever emotions were present as well as any music or sound you remember.

REALIZATIONS

Have you ever had a sudden realization about something, a moment in which an idea, concept or thought comes to you totally out of the blue? With this method of receiving messages, one of two things can occur. First, you formulate a question and the answer immediately pops into your head. Second, you formulate a question, or have something going on in your life on which you desire clarity, and at some unrelated moment an answer or realization pops into your head.

Sudden realizations come quite frequently when you are engaged in non-intellectual or repetitive activities such as chopping vegetable, cleaning the house, showering, folding the laundry, etc. At these times, the logical brain focuses on the task, and the intuitive has the chance to bypass the censoring mechanisms and deliver messages. Like the proverbial light bulb clicking on above the cartoon character's head, an illuminating message shines directly into and through you providing guidance and clarity.

MEDIA

All forms of media provide wonderful opportunities for receiving messages. With a few vacation days available, I decided to visit Disneyworld in Orlando. My only concern was where to stay. My money was limited, and hotels were fairly expensive at that time in Orlando. During the drive from South Carolina to Florida, I began to hum a song. At that moment, I turned on the radio, and the same song was playing at nearly the exact point I had been humming. After I regained my composure, I thought to myself, "What is the message for me here?" The particular song was associated in my mind with a specific friend with whom I had heard it for the first time. Suddenly, I remembered that she lived in Orlando. Once I arrived, I called and received a wonderful invitation to stay while I was in the area. The song had answered my question.

Often, books contain specific messages for us. If you happen to have a question about something, formulate it in your mind. Next, reach for the first book you find and open to a random page. Somewhere on that page will rest a message for you to clarify or answer your question. Certain books to which you are drawn also provide powerful messages. If you find a specific book mentioned repeatedly, recommended by many different people or one that catches your eye at a bookstore, the chances are high that you need to read that book in order to get a message.

While reading, watching television, listening to the radio or experiencing any other media, pay attention to any repeated symbols, patterns or stories. What sticks in your mind? Things that catch your attention in the media very often contain messages for you.

MEDITATION

Old fashioned? Perhaps, but also very effective. Using the *Sacred Space Visualization* from Chapter One, you can receive powerful messages. Formulate the questions or issues on which you desire clarification. Once you enter your sacred space, allow the Universe to send you messages in answer to your questions. The messages might come as visual symbols, sounds, sensations or even literal verbal communication with angels, spirit guides or people on the other side. Pay close attention and journal on anything that occurs.

OTHER PEOPLE

One of the most potent forms for these universal messages comes in the guise of our relationships with other people. Every person with whom we come in contact has some message for us, a gift from Spirit to help us move along our chosen path, even seemingly insignificant or random meetings. These brief, chance encounters provide many potent messages, but more extensive information comes to us through people with whom we have established ongoing relationships.

Some of the most powerful and illuminating messages arrive in the form of people who irritate us. These people invariably mirror something back to you, some energy in your life or personality that has created a "hole" in your energetic shielding. In a later chapter of *Combing The Mirror (and other steps in your spiritual path)* Kevin addresses this concept of other people as mirrors:

"I was once working with a brother and sister. As small children their mother use to take them aside one at a time and tell each one of them that they were her favorite and how much better they were than the other one. Then one or the other child would see 'mama' all affectionate and loving with the other one and feel, on some level, that they had been bad and needed to win back their rightful place. The brother was the older one and learned early how to become very manipulative to win. The sister learned to lie to win back.

"They both grew up and went on to live their own lives, but somewhere the message had registered that one needs to manipulate and lie to guarantee your place in your loved one's affections. Ultimately, what was important was to compete and win.

"When I met them, the brother had gone through three marriages and had a habit of attracting women who clung to him, allowing him to feel superior. He would get caught in pleasing his families (all had children), his current relationship and himself, and would manipulate accordingly. He was currently involved with a woman who would not buy into that, although at times she would admit to 'getting sucked in' and needed to keep her distance.

"The sister was on her second marriage and was constantly triangulating between her daughter from her first marriage and her second husband, her mother and her family, and between her brother and his kids. The children seemed to take turns being estranged from their father (her brother), sometimes his own fault, sometimes from his sister's interference and stretching of the truth. She still had a hard time being honest, especially if she felt under pressure to perform or win.

"The brother and sister had started a business together shortly before I came into the picture, with their mother loaning them the money. This took them back to the original triad, but unfortunately mother decided it was her time to become frail. She was unable to cope and ended up in a nursing home. She was not going to be able to fully play the third role so that these two could once and for all learn their lesson and put it behind them. Conveniently enough, they hired a third person for the business. They discovered within a few months that he was very good at what he did, and in their perception, was needed. But he also was very manipulative and lied. He would alternately buddy up to one, while trashing the other. They soon decided to sell the business.

"Guess what? Nothing seemed to go right. It was almost as if they were stuck with the business. No matter how hard they thought they were trying, they could not quite meet the goals that they needed in order to sell. But once we started talking about how this man was representing everything that they had not yet dealt with from their childhood, it became clearer and clearer to both of them what they needed to face and resolve within themselves. If they did not resolve it and still managed to sell the business, something else would just come along that would put them in the same situation until they learned this lesson.

"Now they were well on their way to changing

their environment. I refer to this as combing the mirror because in a conversation with the brother, trying to explain the nature of change, I came up with this was the exercise to illustrate it.

"The next time you want to change, or fix your environment, go to a mirror and mess up your hair. As you look at your messy hair, take a comb and start combing the mirror. Do that for as long as you need to until you realize that no matter how long or hard or consistently you comb the mirror, your hair will still be messed up. Then stop and think about what you are trying to change or fix in your environment and maybe, just maybe, you will decide that it is time to stop COMBING THE MIRROR."[15]

*****

Exercise

MIRROR, MIRROR ON THE WALL . . .

Revisit you original "Nyah Nyah" list. For each person on that list, ask yourself the following questions:

1.   *What is/was the most annoying thing or pattern about this person?*

2.   *How do I, today, exhibit that same thing, pattern, habit or behavior in my own life?*

If you cannot find any situation in which you exhibit those patterns outwardly, ask the following question:

3.   *How do I exhibit that same thing, pattern, habit or behavior in my internal life, to myself?*

Journal on these issues.

Doing this exercise is not about beating yourself up, so stop it! Only by addressing those areas in which we might be sending out undesirable energy can we then reprogram that energy to attract what we desire. Frankly, you have to turn over a few stones and look at the "dark side" underneath to truly understand your life. Just as you must learn how not to blame others, you must learn not to blame yourself. Remember that blame is a judgemental word. Understanding, acceptance and change can only derive from discernment.

The concept of mirroring need not focus solely on the irritating energy. Many times, we find ourselves drawn to people whom we find to be fabulous company. Their energies inspire us. These people also serve as mirrors. For each person in your life who you find inspiring, inspirational or simply fun to be around ask yourself, "What does this person mirror to me?" Those things that most draw our attention do so because they have a matching energy within us. With this perception, you can help balance any sense of self-recrimination catalyzed by the previous mirroring exercise.

All of the issues discussed in this chapter illustrate ways in which you manifest messages to help you explore, clarify and release issues that block you from achieving spiritual harmony. These energies pass through your shields to facilitate clarity and, ultimately, healing for you.

While working with my Kevin on a joint project, he brought up one additional point that merits consideration. In his words, "Current crisis often turns out to be, in hindsight, a blessing." Many times, energy passes through your shields and appears to be negative, as it has no discernible reason or cause and potentially creates disharmony in your present life. After some time has passed, however, you look back and discover that the energy that appeared so unpleasant was in actuality a blessing.

Consider the following scenario. You have planned a vacation, bought your tickets and made all of the arrangements. At the last moment, your employer has a crisis and cancels your vacation. Since you do not wish to lose your job, you cancel your plans and lose a great deal of money. At the time, you feel ill-used and abused. You might feel anger or resentment at your boss. Certainly, you will feel some sense of being a victim. Several days later, you watch the news and discover that the plane you would have taken crashed, killing everyone aboard. The cancellation of your vacation, in hindsight, becomes a blessing.

The occasional unpleasant experience or painful energy that seemingly passes through our shields despite our best efforts often contains a powerful message for you. You may find in this work that a little time must pass before you can clearly discern all of the messages in any given situation. You must remember the complexity in the web of relationships we all have in our lives. No single experience exists in a vacuum, and thus each incident impacts many things and is, in turn, impacted by many things. You often have to dig a little before uncovering all of the messages that come to you through violation of your boundaries.

As you grow and change, your boundaries will shift with you, often without your conscious knowledge. Universal messages, like those discussed in this chapter, provide you with clues to examine where you might be missing something important or where you might need an adjustment in your shields.

So, on your patience evermore attending,
New joy wait on you! Here our play has ending.

— William Shakespeare, from *Pericles* (V, iii, 101-102)

Chapter 10

Eternal Delight

The title character of Shakespeare's play *Pericles* begins his journey by discovering and speaking a hidden truth. As a result, he endures a journey of rough seas, changeable friendships and chaotic emotions. In the end, however, he sails his ship into a safe harbor and begins a new phase of his life with more wisdom and a greater chance for happiness. As the quote that opens this chapter indicates, "new joy" awaits Pericles once he has reclaimed all things that rightfully belong to him.

Having made it to the concluding chapter of this book, you have probably mirrored the voyage of Pericles metaphorically. You have certainly uncovered and spoken hidden truths in your life. You have probably endured some rough seas, changeable friendships and chaotic emotions. In the end, you too can and will sail your ship into a safe harbor to begin a new phase of life with more wisdom and a greater chance for happiness. "New joy" waits on you as you reclaim the energy that rightfully belongs to you.

To be sure, no journey involving internal change can be completely concluded while you are still in the human form. Life is defined by change. We are in a constant state of energetic flow within ourselves and with all things around us. To stay the same, constant and immovable, can never truly occur while one still exists in the world. Even as you read these words, your energies ebb and flow in such a way that your boundaries shift and change. Each day begins a new journey of discovery, new issues to examine, new people with whom to interact and new energies to experience, filter, absorb and release.

The exercises, visualizations, homework assignments and information presented in this book provide you with a skeletal structure. Once you have put together these pieces, your job then becomes one of personalization. With the foundations constructed, you must then make these processes your own. Adapt the exercises to your own particular issues. Modify the visualizations to suit the flow of your own energy. Expand the homework to encompass issues particular to your own journey.

Most importantly, absorb the information and discern what resonates to you and what does not. As I have said over and over, I do not believe in a larger, cosmic version of truth for everyone, but I do know that each person has his or her personal truth. Hopefully, this book has helped you uncover some of your more powerful personal truths.

The great joy of this work exists in the many blinding flashes of insight, the proverbial "lightbulbs" that click on as you gain greater and greater clarity and focus. As you experience the empowerment of feeling safer and more protected in your life, you can then use your personal energy in more positive ways, to create powerful and transformational change in your life and the lives of everyone around you.

When you have experienced the joy of taking back your life, you truly begin to understand and embrace the profound words of the poet and mystic William Blake:

> *Energy is the only life and is from the Body . . .*
> *Energy is Eternal Delight.*

*****

Enjoy the eternal delight of your journey!

Endnotes

Chapter One

1.   Smil, Vaclav. *General Energetics: Energy in the Biosphere and Civilization.* (New York: John Wiley & Sons, 1991), p. vii.

2.   Eddington, Sir Arthur Stanley. *Science and the Unseen World.* (New York: Macmillan, 1929.)

Chapter Two

3.   Sommer, Robert. *Personal Space: The Behavioral Basis of Design.* (Englewood Cliffs, NJ: Prentice Hall, 1969), p. 27.

4.   Freedman, Jonathan L. *Crowding and Behavior.* (New York: The Viking Press, 1975), p.73.

5.   Sommer, p. 27.

6.   Pierrakos, John. "The Human Energy Field." *The Energies of Consciousness: Explorations In Acupuncture, Auras and Kirlian Photography.* Stanley Krippner and Daniel Rubin, ed. (New York: Interface, 1975), p. 161.

7.   Sommer, p. 29.

Chapter Six

8.   Mercer, Johnny and Harold Arlen. "Accentuate The Positive." 1941.

Chapter Seven

9.   Lapine, James and Stephen Sondheim. *Sunday In The Park With George.* (New York: Applause Theatre Book Publishers, 1991).

Chapter Eight

10.   Lamott, Anne. *Crooked Little Heart.* (New York: Pantheon Books, 1997.)

11.   Lawrence, Jerome and Robert E. Lee. *Inherit The Wind.* (New York: Bantam Books, 1960), p. 66.

12.   Delille, Jacques. *Malheur et Pitié*, 1803. Canto 1.

Chapter Nine

13.   Emery, Kevin Ross. *Combing The Mirror (and other steps in your spiritual path).* (Portsmouth, NH: LightLines Publishing, 1998), p. 131.

14.   Emery, pp. 111-112.

15.   Emery, pp. 129-131.

Glossary

BELIEF: An idea or concept generated in part by another person and which can be altered as a result of outside influence.

DISCERNMENT: Knowing what is right or wrong for you.

EMPATHY: The capacity for projecting oneself into another's energy, thereby achieving a sympathetic understanding of someone.

EMPOWERMENT: The power to be uniquely who you are without apology.

JOY: Being completely present in the moment, allowing yourself to have your emotions in totality, expressing them fully.

JUDGEMENT: Taking what is right or wrong for you and trying to make it right or wrong for someone else.

KNOWING: An idea or concept that is an integral part of your reality, one that is not subject to outside influence.

NEED: Something essential to survival.

NEGATIVITY: Energy that is intentionally designed to cause harm.

RIGHT: Something that is harmonious with your spiritual path, which helps you feel centered and joyful.

SANCTIMONY: The judgemental assumption that what is right or wrong for you is the only truth and all other truths are less valid.

SELF-JUDGEMENT: Seeing what is right or wrong for someone else and trying to make it right or wrong for you, regardless of your own knowing.

SYMPATHY: The fact or power of sharing the feelings of another, especially in sorrow or trouble; fellow feeling, compassion or commiseration.

WRONG: Anything that does not feel harmonious with your spiritual path, and causes you to feel off-center and unhappy.

Selected Bibliography

Bateson, Gregory. *Mind and Nature.* New York: Dutton, 1979.

Bertalanffy, Ludwig von. *General Systems Theory: Foundations, Development, Applications.* New York: George Braziller, 1968.

Burr, Harold Saxton. *Blueprint for Immortality: The Electric Patterns of Life.* London: Neville Spearman, 1972.

Cameron, Julia. *The Artist's Way: A Spiritual Path to Higher Creativity.* New York: G.P. Putnam's Sons, 1992.

Campbell, Joseph. *The Hero with a Thousand Faces*, second edition. Princeton, NJ: Princeton University Press, 1968.

Capra, Fritjof. *The Tao of Physics.* Berkley: Shambhala, 1975.

Capra, Fritjof. *The Turning Point: Science, Society and the Rising Culture.* New York: Bantam Books, 1982.

Combs, Allan and Mark Holland. *Synchronicity: Science, Myth and the Trickster.* New York: Marlowe and Company, 1996.

Davis, Mark H. *Empathy: A Social Psychological Approach.* Boulder, CO: Westview Press, 1996.

Dobrin, Richard et al. "Experimental Measurements of the Human Energy Field." *The Energies of Consciousness: Explorations In Acupuncture, Auras and Kirlian Photography*, Stanley Krippner and Daniel Rubin, ed. New York: Interface, 1975.

Eddington, Sir Arthur Stanley. *Science and the Unseen World.* New York: Macmillan, 1929.

Edwards, Betty. *Drawing on the Right Side of the Brain.* Los Angeles: Jeremy P. Tarcher, Inc., 1989.

Emery, Kevin Ross. *Combing The Mirror (and other steps in your spiritual path).* Portsmouth, NH: LightLines Publishing, 1998.

Emery, Kevin Ross and Thomas A. Hensel. *Experiment Earth: Journey Back To The Beginning.* Portsmouth, NH: LightLines Publishing, 1999.

Felipe, N.J. and Robert Sommer. "Invasion of Personal Space," *Social Problems*, 14 (1966), pp. 206 – 214.

Fellow, Deborah, ed. *Setting Boundaries: The Anthropology of Spatial and Social Organization.* Westport, CT: Bergin & Garvey, 1996.

Fogelman, Betsy, ed. *The Oriental Medicine Research Guide.* Santa Fe, NM: In Word Press, 1993.

Freedman, Jonathan L. *Crowding and Behavior.* New York: The Viking Press, 1975.

Freeman, Dyson. *From Eros to Gaia.* New York: Pantheon Books, 1992.

Grad, Bernard. "Healing By the Laying on of Hands: A Review of Experiments." *Ways of Health: Holistic Approaches to Ancient and Contemporary Medicine.* David Sobel, ed. New York: Harcourt, Brace Jovanovich, 1979.

Green, Elmer and Alyce. *Beyond Biofeedback.* San Francisco: Delacorte Press, 1977.

Hall, Edward T. *The Hidden Dimension.* New York: Doubleday & Company, Inc. 1966.

Heisenberg, Werner. *Physics and Philosophy*. New York: Harper & Row, 1962.

Hensel, Thomas A. and Kevin Ross Emery. *The Lost Steps of Reiki: The Channeled Teachings of Wei Chi*. Portsmouth, NH: LightLines Publishing, 1997.

Hoff, Benjamin. *The Tao of Pooh*. New York: Penguin Books, 1983.

Insel, Paul M. and Henry Clay Lindgren. *Too Close For Comfort*. Englewood Cliffs, NJ: Prentice Hall, 1978.

Jantsch, Erich. *The Self-Organizing Universe*. New York: Pergamon, 1980.

Judith, Anodea. *Wheels of Life: A User's Guide to the Chakra System*. St. Paul, MN: Llewellyn Publications, 1987.

Keleman, Stanley. *Your Body Speaks Its Mind*. Berkeley, CA: Center Press, 1981.

Koestler, Arthur. *Janus*. London: Hutchinson, 1978.

Kuhn, Thomas S. *The Structure of Scientific Revolution*. Chicago: University of Chicago Press, 1970.

Krieger, Dolores. *The Therapeutic Touch: How to Use Your Hands to Help or to Heal*. New York: Prentice Hall, 1979.

Lawrence, Jerome and Robert E. Lee. *Inherit The Wind*. New York: Bantam Books, 1960.

Lowen, Alexander, M.D. *Bioenergetics*. New York: Penguin Books, 1975.

Lundberg, Paul. *The Book of Shiatsu*. London: Gaia Books, 1992.

Ostriker, Patricia, ed. *William Blake: The Complete Poems*. New York: Penguin Books, 1977.

Pert, Candace B. *Molecules of Emotion: Why You Feel the Way You Feel.* New York: Scribner, 1997.

Pierrakos, John. "The Human Energy Field." *The Energies of Consciousness: Explorations In Acupuncture, Auras and Kirlian Photography.* Stanley Krippner and Daniel Rubin, ed. New York: Interface, 1975.

Porkert, Manfred. *The Theoretical Foundation of Chinese Medicine: Systems of Correspondence.* Cambridge, MA: The MIT Press, 1974.

Redfield, James. *The Celestine Prophecy.* New York: Warner Books, 1993.

Reich, Wilhelm. *Beyond Psychology: Letters and Journals, 1934 – 1935.* Mary Boyd Higgins, editor. Derek and Inge Jordan and Philip Schwartz, trans. New York: Farrar, Strauss & Giroux, 1994.

Reich, Wilhelm. *The Discovery of the Orgone, volume 1.* Theodore P. Wolfe, trans. New York: The Noonday Press, 1961.

Reich, Wilhelm. *Selected Writings.* New York: Farrar, Straus & Giroux, 1979.

Sanford, Agnes. *God Works Through Us.* St. Paul, MN: Macalester Park Publishing Co., 1947.

Simonton, O. Carl, Stephanie Matthews-Simonton and James Creighton. *Getting Well Again.* Los Angeles: Tarcher, 1978.

Smil, Vaclav. *General Energetics: Energy in the Biosphere and Civilization.* New York: John Wiley & Sons, 1991.

Sommer, Robert. *Personal Space: The Behavioral Basis of Design.* Englewood Cliffs, NJ: Prentice Hall, 1969.

Sorokin, Pitrim A. *Social and Cultural Dynamics*, 4 volumes. New York: American Book Co., 1937 – 1941.

Stace, Walter T. *The Teachings of the Mystics*. New York: New American Library, 1960.

Talbot, Michael. *The Holographic Universe*. New York, Harper Collins, 1991.

Thie, John F., D.C. *Touch For Health: a new approach to restoring our natural energies*, revised edition. Marina del Rey, CA: DeVorss Company, 1994.

Toynbee, Arnold. *A Study of History*. New York: Oxford University Press, 1972.

Vithoulkas, George. *The Science of Homeopathy*. New York: Grove, 1980.

Wilbur, Ken, ed. *Quantum Questions: Mystical Writings of the World's Great Physicists*. Boston: Shambhala, 1984.

Yasuo, Yuasa. *The Body, Self-Cultivation, And Ki-Energy*. Shigenori Nagatomo and Monty S. Hull, trans. New York: State University of New York Press, 1993.

About the Author

Rev. Tommy Hensel, D. Div

A resident of Portsmouth, New Hampshire, Rev. Tommy Hensel maintains a full-time practice as spiritual coach and counselor. He has worked with hundreds of people both privately and in workshops to transform their lives utilizing the techniques described in this book. Along with his partner Rev. Kevin Ross Emery, Tommy is one of the creators and teachers of the *Wei Chi Tibetan Reiki*™ system of natural healing. This system is based on information channeled through Kevin by Wei Chi, a 5,000-year-old Tibetan shaman and one of the original creators of the healing system from which the modern practice of Reiki was extracted.

Tommy holds a B.A. in Communication and a B.A. in Music from Florida State University, an M.A. in Theatre from the University of South Carolina, and both a Masters and a Doctorate in Divinity from the Universal Brotherhood University. He is a Minister/Director in the Universal Brotherhood Movement, an interfaith ministry, and is a Feng Shui practitioner.

He is the co-author of three audio tapes *Prosperity & Manifestation, The Lost Steps of Reiki: Transforming An Ancient Healing Art* and *The Channeled Teachings of Simon Peter*, and two books *The Lost Steps of Reiki: The Channeled Teachings of Wei Chi* and *Experiment Earth: Journey Back To The Beginning*. Both Tommy and Kevin maintain a heavy schedule of travelling, speaking and lecturing both nationally and internationally.

For more information on ordering books and tapes, or to reach any *LightLines Publishing* author, please direct your inquiries to:

LightLines Publishing
One Middle Street
Portsmouth, NH   03801-4301

LightLinesPub@aol.com

http://www.weboflight.com/publish.htm